The Hi

From Antiquity to Today

Land of Origins: Introduction to Ethiopia's Ancient Past

Nestled within the northeastern corner of Africa, Ethiopia stands as a testament to the origins of human civilization and the richness of its ancient past. Its history stretches back beyond recorded time, revealing a mosaic of cultures, civilizations, and landscapes that have shaped the destiny of this remarkable land.

Ethiopia's significance transcends its geographic borders. Fossils discovered in the country have provided crucial insights into the evolution of early humans. The most famous among them, the partial skeleton of "Lucy" (Australopithecus afarensis), was found in the Afar region in 1974, offering an incredible glimpse into the distant past of our species.

But it's not just paleontological findings that underline Ethiopia's role as a cradle of civilization. The region's history is deeply intertwined with the Kingdom of Aksum, which emerged around the 4th century BCE and extended its influence across the Red Sea to southern Arabia and the Mediterranean. The Aksumites, known for their mastery of trade, erected towering obelisks and established trade routes that connected their empire to the farthest corners of the ancient world.

A significant aspect of Ethiopia's identity is its religious heritage. The introduction of Christianity to the region is believed to have occurred in the 4th century CE during the reign of King Ezana of Aksum. The country's strong connection to the Christian faith is evident in its unique form of Christianity, Ethiopian Orthodox Tewahedo Church, which holds a distinctive place in the global Christian community. The ancient city of Lalibela, known for its rock-hewn churches, stands as a testament to this spiritual legacy.

The Zagwe Dynasty, which succeeded the Aksumites, left a lasting mark on Ethiopian history. The construction of the rock-hewn churches of Lalibela occurred during this era, showcasing both the architectural prowess and religious fervor of the time. The dynasty's rule also saw the establishment of a flourishing civilization that contributed to the country's cultural tapestry.

It's crucial to acknowledge the complexity of Ethiopia's history, including periods of conflict and change. The Solomonic Dynasty, tracing its lineage to the biblical King Solomon and the Queen of Sheba, played a central role in the nation's medieval history. However, the region also experienced external pressures, including incursions by various European powers seeking to establish dominance in the Horn of Africa.

Ethiopia's resistance against colonial ambitions reached a defining moment during the Battle of Adwa in 1896, where the Ethiopian forces successfully repelled an Italian invasion, becoming a symbol of African resilience against imperialism. This victory made Ethiopia the only African country to avoid colonization during the "Scramble for Africa."

As we embark on this journey through Ethiopia's ancient past, it's important to recognize the interplay of diverse cultures, the preservation of ancient traditions, and the enduring legacy of this land. From its paleontological treasures to its magnificent architectural wonders, Ethiopia's history offers a glimpse into the earliest chapters of human civilization and provides a foundation for understanding the intricate tapestry of cultures that have flourished within its borders.

The Enigma of Lucy: Prehistoric Ethiopia and Human Origins

In the realm of human origins, Ethiopia emerges as a captivating treasure trove, offering a window into the distant past through the fossils and remnants of our ancient ancestors. One such remarkable find, the partial skeleton of "Lucy," has unveiled tantalizing insights into the evolution of early humans and the unfolding story of our species.

Discovered in 1974 by paleoanthropologist Donald Johanson in the Afar region of Ethiopia, Lucy's remains belong to Australopithecus afarensis, a hominid species that lived approximately 3.2 million years ago. Named after the Beatles' song "Lucy in the Sky with Diamonds," the significance of this discovery cannot be overstated. It provides a crucial link in the chain of human evolution, bridging the gap between apes and modern humans.

Lucy's fossilized skeleton, though incomplete, has offered profound insights into the bipedal nature of these early hominids. Her pelvic structure and the alignment of her knee and hip joints indicate a posture suitable for upright walking, a defining characteristic of our human lineage. This adaptation to walking on two legs marked a pivotal shift in hominid evolution, freeing up the hands for tool use and other complex activities.

The fossil record of Australopithecus afarensis, of which Lucy is the most famous example, has enabled researchers to piece together a more comprehensive understanding of our ancient relatives. With their relatively small cranial capacity and elongated arms, they likely occupied a niche between tree-dwelling primates and later, more advanced hominid species. This delicate balancing act between arboreal and terrestrial lifestyles sheds light on the dynamic environmental pressures that shaped their adaptations.

Ethiopia's role as a hub for paleontological discoveries extends beyond Lucy's fame. The Afar region, where Lucy was found, has yielded numerous other hominid remains and artifacts that contribute to our understanding of human evolution. The region's geological conditions have played a crucial role in preserving these ancient remnants, providing a rare glimpse into the lives of our distant ancestors.

However, interpreting these remnants is not without its challenges. The gaps in the fossil record and the limited number of specimens make it difficult to create a complete picture of the Australopithecus afarensis population. Additionally, debates persist about the extent of their cognitive abilities, social structures, and interactions with their environment. These uncertainties drive ongoing research, inviting scientists to piece together the puzzle of our origins.

As we peer back through the corridors of time, the story of Lucy and her kin underscores the complexities of evolution and the gradual transformations that paved the way for the emergence of modern humans. Ethiopia's role as a cradle of humanity continues to captivate researchers and enthusiasts alike, offering a humbling reminder of our shared origins and the intricacies that shaped our journey from ancient apes to the remarkable beings we are today.

Kingdom of Aksum: Rise of a Mighty Civilization

In the heart of Ethiopia's ancient landscape, a kingdom emerged that would leave an indelible mark on the history of Africa and the world. The Kingdom of Aksum, also spelled Axum, rose to prominence around the 4th century BCE and would flourish for over a millennium, becoming a powerful and influential civilization that commanded respect and admiration.

Located in the northern part of modern-day Ethiopia, Aksum's strategic positioning along trade routes linking the Red Sea to the Mediterranean and India allowed it to harness the wealth of international commerce. This advantageous location facilitated the exchange of goods, ideas, and cultures, elevating Aksum to a position of global significance. The kingdom's prosperity was deeply intertwined with its mastery of trade, and it controlled key ports such as Adulis that enabled access to the vast Indian Ocean network.

One of Aksum's most iconic symbols was its towering obelisks, carved from single pieces of granite and adorned with intricate designs. These obelisks, known as stelae, stood as both markers of prestige and symbols of the kingdom's religious beliefs. The largest of these stelae, known as the "Obelisk of Axum," stood at over 100 feet tall and remains one of the tallest monolithic structures ever erected.

Aksum's rulers were known for their grand ambitions and accomplishments. King Ezana, in particular, left an enduring legacy. His conversion to Christianity in the 4th century CE, making Aksum one of the earliest Christian kingdoms, marked a significant turning point in the history of the region. The introduction of Christianity transformed the cultural and religious landscape, leaving an indelible imprint on Ethiopia's identity.

The civilization's wealth was also demonstrated through its impressive architecture and engineering feats. The "Stelae Park" in Aksum contains a collection of obelisks, many of which were toppled over time. These monuments not only reflected the kingdom's prominence but also its engineering prowess in quarrying, transporting, and erecting these colossal stone structures.

Another testament to Aksum's grandeur is the archaeological site of Aksum's royal palace, which offers glimpses into the opulent lifestyle of its rulers. The palace complex showcases well-constructed buildings, intricate decorations, and courtyards that provide insights into the kingdom's artistry and urban planning.

The Kingdom of Aksum also maintained a vibrant culture. It is credited with developing its own script, Ge'ez, which played a crucial role in the preservation of the kingdom's history and cultural heritage. The written records of Aksum provide invaluable insights into its governance, religious practices, and societal norms.

As the centuries passed, Aksum's influence waned due to a variety of factors, including shifts in trade routes and the rise of neighboring powers. Despite its decline, the kingdom's legacy endured through the establishment of the

Ethiopian Orthodox Tewahedo Church, its architectural wonders, and its contributions to the development of Ge'ez script.

The rise and fall of the Kingdom of Aksum stand as a testament to the ebb and flow of civilizations. Its legacy continues to be celebrated not only as an integral part of Ethiopian history but also as a beacon of African achievement and cultural significance. The echoes of Aksum's greatness resonate through the ages, reminding us of the remarkable achievements that can arise from the confluence of strategic positioning, cultural innovation, and human ingenuity.

Obelisks and Trade Routes: Aksum's Global Influence

Within the heart of Ethiopia's historical landscape, the Kingdom of Aksum flourished as a beacon of global influence, propelled by its strategic position and mastery of trade routes. The kingdom's rise to prominence was intrinsically tied to its control over these vital conduits of commerce, and its legacy is etched in the monumental obelisks that marked its presence and the far-reaching trade networks it nurtured.

The towering obelisks of Aksum stand as testaments to the kingdom's grandeur and architectural prowess. Carved from single pieces of granite, these monolithic structures soared skyward, their polished surfaces reflecting not only the sun's rays but also the magnificence of the civilization that created them. The obelisks, or stelae, served multiple purposes in Aksumite society. They were markers of prestige, signaling important sites such as royal tombs, and also had religious significance, serving as symbols of the sun god and fertility.

However, the obelisks were more than mere symbols; they were manifestations of the kingdom's extensive influence over trade networks that spanned continents. Aksum's strategic location, situated between the Red Sea and the Mediterranean, positioned it at the crossroads of global commerce. The port city of Adulis, under Aksum's control, became a thriving hub that connected the Indian Ocean maritime routes with the bustling markets of the Mediterranean.

Through these trade connections, Aksum accumulated vast wealth and exerted influence on a global scale. Precious commodities such as ivory, gold, frankincense, and myrrh flowed through its ports, enriching the kingdom and enhancing its standing in the wider world. Aksum's demand for exotic goods was met by trading partners from India, Arabia, Persia, and the Mediterranean, creating a vibrant exchange of not just material goods, but also cultural ideas and practices.

The kingdom's maritime dominance was further underscored by its naval prowess. Aksum maintained a formidable fleet that safeguarded its maritime routes and ensured the flow of trade. These naval capabilities enabled Aksum to extend its influence to the Arabian Peninsula and establish control over parts of southern Arabia, creating a symbiotic relationship between the kingdom and its trading partners.

Aksum's global reach is also reflected in its coinage. The Aksumite currency, minted from gold and silver, was widely accepted in trade networks spanning the Red Sea and beyond. This currency played a crucial role in facilitating trade and solidifying the kingdom's economic strength.

The decline of Aksum's obelisks and its global influence can be attributed to a combination of factors. Shifts in trade routes, environmental changes, and the rise of competing powers all played a role in shaping the kingdom's destiny. Despite its eventual decline, Aksum's legacy endures through the remnants of its obelisks, the archaeological records, and its impact on the region's cultural and religious development.

As we reflect on Aksum's global influence, we are reminded of the interconnectedness of civilizations and the power of strategic positioning in shaping history. The obelisks, those towering sentinels of Aksum's glory, stand as timeless witnesses to a civilization that carved its mark not only in stone but also in the annals of world history, leaving an enduring legacy that continues to captivate and inspire.

Rock-Hewn Wonders: Lalibela's Architectural Marvels

In the rugged highlands of Ethiopia lies a place of awe-inspiring beauty and architectural mastery: the town of Lalibela. Renowned for its rock-hewn churches, Lalibela stands as a testament to human ingenuity, devotion, and the enduring connection between faith and the built environment. These subterranean sanctuaries have captured the imagination of travelers, historians, and architects alike, offering a glimpse into a world where spirituality and artistry converged to create a unique architectural legacy.

The story of Lalibela's rock-hewn wonders unfolds against the backdrop of medieval Ethiopia, during the reign of King Lalibela in the 12th century. The king's vision was driven by a desire to establish a "New Jerusalem," a holy site that could rival the spiritual significance of the Holy Land. The result was an ambitious endeavor: a complex of monolithic churches hewn from solid rock, meticulously carved into the earth.

The Lalibela complex comprises eleven rock-hewn churches, each with its own distinct design and architectural features. Carved directly into the bedrock, these structures are more than just places of worship; they are feats of engineering and artistic expression that have stood the test of time. The churches are divided into two groups, symbolizing the earthly and heavenly realms, with a network of tunnels, passageways, and courtyards connecting them.

The Church of St. George, arguably the most iconic of Lalibela's churches, captures the imagination with its intricate cross-shaped design. Carved entirely below ground level, it is accessed through a trench-like corridor that opens into a sunken courtyard. The church itself resembles a cross when viewed from above, with its walls adorned with intricately carved windows, arches, and decorative motifs.

The attention to detail in Lalibela's churches is awe-inspiring. The monolithic pillars, meticulously carved ceilings, and symbolic designs reflect the convergence of artistic expression and spiritual devotion. Many of the churches feature delicate carvings that tell biblical stories and depict saints, angels, and other religious figures.

The techniques employed in the creation of these architectural wonders are a testament to the skilled craftsmanship of the time. The carvers used primitive tools such as chisels and hammers to painstakingly shape the rock, turning the natural landscape into a sanctuary of spiritual significance. The level of precision achieved in these carvings speaks volumes about the dedication and artistry of the artisans who shaped them.

Lalibela's rock-hewn churches continue to serve as active places of worship and pilgrimage, drawing both local devotees and curious travelers from around the world. The annual Timket festival, celebrating Epiphany, sees the churches bustling with faithful pilgrims, adding a vibrancy and vitality that resonates with the history that lies within their stone walls.

As we explore Lalibela's architectural marvels, we are invited to contemplate the profound connection between human aspiration, faith, and creativity. The rock-hewn churches of Lalibela stand as a testament to the power of vision and the human capacity to shape the physical world in service of the spiritual. They serve as reminders that even in the harshest of landscapes, the human spirit can carve out spaces of beauty, meaning, and transcendence.

Zagwe Dynasty: Legacy of Lalibela and Beyond

The Zagwe Dynasty, a significant chapter in Ethiopian history, emerged as the successor to the Aksumite Kingdom and played a pivotal role in shaping the nation's cultural, architectural, and religious landscape. Centered around the town of Lalibela, the dynasty's legacy is intimately intertwined with the architectural marvels of the rock-hewn churches, bearing witness to an era of creativity, spiritual devotion, and the continuity of Ethiopia's rich heritage.

The Zagwe Dynasty's rise to power is shrouded in historical complexity. It is believed to have originated in the 10th century CE and is named after its founder, King Zagwe. While its precise origins are debated, the dynasty's influence became more pronounced under the reign of King Lalibela, after whom the town and its iconic churches are named. King Lalibela is believed to have played a central role in the creation of the rock-hewn churches, envisioning them as a "New Jerusalem" and a center of religious pilgrimage.

The dynasty's legacy is most famously associated with the rock-hewn churches of Lalibela, a testament to the spiritual and architectural aspirations of the time. These subterranean sanctuaries, hewn from solid rock, not only served as places of worship but also as symbols of the Zagwe rulers' religious devotion and their ambition to establish a lasting spiritual legacy. The rock-hewn churches of Lalibela are a testament to the dynasty's patronage of the arts and their commitment to weaving faith into the fabric of the landscape.

Beyond the architectural wonders, the Zagwe Dynasty's legacy extended to governance, culture, and religion. While Lalibela's rock-hewn churches are the most visible aspect of this legacy, the dynasty's influence permeated various aspects of Ethiopian society. The dynasty's capital, Roha, later known as Lalibela, became a hub of cultural exchange and religious scholarship, attracting scholars, pilgrims, and artists from near and far.

The Zagwe Dynasty's significance is reflected in its impact on the Ethiopian Orthodox Tewahedo Church. Under the dynasty's rule, the church's influence expanded, with the creation of monastic communities and the establishment of religious institutions that played a vital role in preserving and propagating Ethiopia's Christian traditions.

However, the Zagwe Dynasty's reign was not without its challenges and conflicts. The establishment of the dynasty marked a departure from the Solomonic lineage that had ruled Aksum and raised questions about the legitimacy of its rule. This led to tensions and conflicts with other factions that considered themselves the rightful rulers of Ethiopia. These disputes laid the groundwork for the eventual resurgence of the Solomonic Dynasty, leading to a complex interplay of power dynamics.

As the Zagwe Dynasty eventually gave way to the reestablishment of the Solomonic Dynasty, its legacy endured through the rock-hewn churches of Lalibela and the cultural and religious influences it left behind. The dynasty's period of rule serves as a testament to the resilience of Ethiopian identity, the continuity of Christian traditions, and the capacity of visionary rulers to leave a lasting imprint on the landscape and history of a nation.

The legacy of the Zagwe Dynasty is a reminder of the interplay between power, culture, and spirituality. It underscores the enduring impact that a dynasty can have, not only through the institutions it establishes but also through the architectural marvels and cultural expressions that bear its name. The Zagwe Dynasty's story is a continuation of Ethiopia's intricate narrative, revealing the complex tapestry of its history and the threads that bind its past to its present.

Gondar: The Camelot of Africa's Highlands

In the highlands of Ethiopia, a city emerged that would capture the imagination and evoke comparisons to legendary realms: Gondar, often referred to as the "Camelot of Africa's Highlands." Nestled against the backdrop of the Simien Mountains, Gondar's legacy is one of architectural splendor, cultural vibrancy, and a royal court that left an indelible mark on Ethiopia's history.

Gondar's rise to prominence took place during the reign of Emperor Fasilides in the 17th century. The emperor sought to establish a new capital that would reflect his grand ambitions and foster a sense of royal authority. The result was the creation of Gondar, a city that would serve as the political, cultural, and architectural center of Ethiopia for generations to come.

At the heart of Gondar's allure is its breathtaking architectural heritage. The city is renowned for its collection of castles, palaces, and churches, all constructed during a relatively short span of time. These structures stand as testaments to the artistic prowess and vision of the time, combining Ethiopian architectural traditions with diverse influences from the Middle East, Europe, and India.

The focal point of Gondar's architectural ensemble is the Royal Enclosure, a sprawling complex that houses a series of majestic castles and palaces. Each structure boasts unique design elements, ranging from Indian-inspired arches and Moorish-style domes to indigenous Ethiopian influences. The castles were not only symbols of imperial power but also served as functional residences and administrative centers.

Among the most celebrated structures within the Royal Enclosure is Fasil Ghebbi, Emperor Fasilides' own palace. The palace complex is a microcosm of architectural diversity, with its open-air bathing pool, ceremonial halls, and intricate frescoes that adorn the walls. The architecture of Fasil Ghebbi reflects the cultural crosscurrents of the time, as well as the empire's desire to create a distinct identity that resonated with both local and international influences.

Gondar's significance extended beyond architecture. The city's thriving cultural scene was nurtured by the presence of scholars, poets, artists, and religious figures who were drawn to the royal court. Gondar's cultural vibrancy was further enhanced by its position as a crossroads of trade and diplomacy, facilitating the exchange of ideas, art, and knowledge.

Religion played a central role in Gondar's identity. The city is home to a collection of churches, some of which have played integral roles in Ethiopian Christianity for centuries. Debre Birhan Selassie Church, adorned with its famous ceiling of angelic faces, is one such architectural gem that continues to inspire awe and devotion.

As with any vibrant historical city, Gondar's legacy is not without its complexities. The decline of the city's prominence was marked by internal conflicts, external invasions, and shifting centers of power. However, Gondar's imprint on Ethiopian history remains enduring, as seen in the continued reverence for its architectural wonders, its influence on the broader cultural landscape, and its place as a symbol of Ethiopia's past grandeur.

Gondar, the "Camelot of Africa's Highlands," stands as a reminder of the intersection of art, culture, and political ambition. Its architectural splendor reflects the dynamism and cosmopolitan nature of Ethiopian society during the 17th and 18th centuries. The echoes of Gondar's greatness continue to reverberate through time, inviting us to explore the threads that connect past and present, and to marvel at the enduring allure of a city that once served as a glittering jewel in Ethiopia's crown.

Solomonic Dynasty: Myth, History, and Rule

The Solomonic Dynasty, an enduring and deeply revered lineage in Ethiopian history, weaves together myth, history, and governance into a tapestry that has shaped the nation's identity for centuries. Anchored in the belief that its rulers are descendants of King Solomon and the Queen of Sheba, this dynasty has left an indelible mark on Ethiopia's cultural, religious, and political landscape.

The origins of the Solomonic Dynasty are shrouded in myth and legend. According to Ethiopian tradition, the dynasty traces its lineage to the biblical King Solomon and the Queen of Sheba, who, as the story goes, visited Solomon in Jerusalem and bore him a son, Menelik I. This lineage, believed to be unbroken for thousands of years, forms the bedrock of the dynasty's legitimacy and the spiritual connection between Ethiopia and ancient Israel.

While the dynastic origin story may be shrouded in myth, its historical roots are well documented. The Solomonic Dynasty gained prominence in the 13th century with the rise of Yekuno Amlak, who sought to restore the Solomonic lineage to power after a period of regional fragmentation. Yekuno Amlak's reign marked the beginning of the dynasty's formal rule, and his actions were seen as a fulfillment of the prophecies that foretold the return of the Solomonic monarchy.

The Solomonic rulers governed Ethiopia under a system known as "Zemene Mesafint," which translates to "Era of the Princes." This era was characterized by a decentralization of power, with regional nobles wielding considerable influence. While the Solomonic monarchs maintained their symbolic and spiritual authority, the political landscape was marked by power struggles, local autonomy, and shifting alliances among the nobility.

One of the most renowned figures of the Solomonic Dynasty is Emperor Haile Selassie I, who ruled from 1930 to 1974. Haile Selassie's reign witnessed a period of modernization and reform, aimed at modernizing Ethiopia's institutions and integrating the nation into the international community. His efforts included the introduction of a constitution, educational reforms, and efforts to modernize the economy.

However, the Solomonic Dynasty's rule was not without challenges. The era of the "Zemene Mesafint" was marked by internal conflicts and regional rivalries that often hindered effective governance. Additionally, external pressures, including Italian invasion attempts in the late 19th and early 20th centuries, tested the dynasty's resilience and its ability to protect Ethiopia's sovereignty.

The Solomonic Dynasty's religious significance cannot be understated. Ethiopian Orthodoxy, deeply intertwined with the dynasty's legitimacy, played a central role in the nation's cultural and spiritual identity. The Ethiopian Orthodox Tewahedo Church served as a unifying force, anchoring the nation's sense of continuity and linking it to its ancient heritage.

The fall of the Solomonic Dynasty in 1974 marked a new chapter in Ethiopia's history. Emperor Haile Selassie's rule was brought to an end by a military coup, leading to the establishment of a Marxist-Leninist regime known as the Derg. This period marked a significant departure from the centuries-old tradition of Solomonic rule and initiated a period of social, political, and economic transformation.

The Solomonic Dynasty's legacy endures in Ethiopia's collective memory, cultural expressions, and the ongoing reverence for its historical role. Its influence extends beyond the realm of governance, shaping the nation's art, literature, and spiritual practices. The dynasty's story is a testament to the enduring power of myth, the complexities of historical reality, and the interplay between symbolic authority and tangible governance. As Ethiopia continues to evolve, the Solomonic Dynasty remains an integral thread in the fabric of the nation's narrative, reminding us of the dynamic interplay between myth and history that defines its identity.

Adal Sultanate: Conflict and Confluence with Islam

In the historical tapestry of the Horn of Africa, the Adal Sultanate emerges as a significant chapter marked by the interplay between Islam, regional politics, and cross-cultural influences. Founded in the 13th century, the Adal Sultanate's rise to prominence was driven by its embrace of Islam and its complex interactions with neighboring powers, resulting in a legacy that is both fascinating and complex.

The origins of the Adal Sultanate can be traced back to the 13th century, when Muslim leaders sought to establish a realm that would serve as a bastion of Islam in the region. This endeavor was a response to the spread of Islam in the Horn of Africa and the desire to create a political entity that aligned with the faith's teachings and values.

The Sultanate's capital, Zeila, became a center of trade, scholarship, and Islamic culture. Positioned along important trade routes, Zeila facilitated the exchange of goods, ideas, and knowledge between the Arabian Peninsula, the Indian Ocean, and the African hinterland. The city's prominence drew merchants, scholars, and religious leaders, contributing to its cosmopolitan character.

The embrace of Islam became a defining aspect of the Adal Sultanate's identity. Islamic scholars and institutions flourished within its borders, and Zeila's mosques and madrasas became centers of learning and religious practice. The spread of Islam not only shaped the cultural fabric of the Sultanate but also influenced its governance, legal systems, and societal norms.

The Adal Sultanate's interactions with neighboring powers were marked by both cooperation and conflict. One of its most significant rivals was the Christian Kingdom of Abyssinia, known as Ethiopia. The Adal Sultanate's expansionist ambitions and its commitment to Islam created tensions with the Christian kingdom, leading to a series of conflicts that would shape the geopolitical landscape of the region.

One of the most notable conflicts between the Adal Sultanate and Ethiopia was the Abyssinian-Adal War, also known as the "War of the Conquest." This protracted conflict spanned several decades and was characterized by a series of military engagements and shifting alliances. The rivalry between the two powers was fueled by religious differences, territorial disputes, and struggles for dominance in the region.

During this conflict, the Adal Sultanate received support from the Ottoman Empire, which saw an opportunity to expand its influence in the Red Sea region. The Ottoman support bolstered the Sultanate's military capabilities and allowed it to challenge Abyssinian dominance. However, the prolonged conflict took a toll on both sides and contributed to a period of instability and upheaval.

The Adal Sultanate's decline was precipitated by a combination of factors, including internal divisions, external pressures, and changing power dynamics. Its ambitions were further hindered by the rise of the Portuguese in the region, who sought to establish control over maritime trade routes.

While the Adal Sultanate eventually fell to the combined forces of the Ottoman Empire and Abyssinia, its legacy endures as a testament to the complex interplay between faith, politics, and cultural interactions. The Sultanate's embrace of Islam left an indelible mark on the Horn of Africa, contributing to the region's diverse religious landscape. Its conflicts with Abyssinia underscore the intricate web of historical rivalries and the enduring influence of geopolitics on the course of history.

The Adal Sultanate's story serves as a reminder of the complexities inherent in the historical narratives of the Horn of Africa. It highlights the region's role as a crossroads of cultures, religions, and political ambitions, showcasing the ever-evolving dynamics that have shaped its history. The Sultanate's legacy invites us to explore the intersections of faith and power, the impact of external influences, and the intricate relationships that have defined the Horn of Africa's historical trajectory.

The Portuguese Connection: Early European Interactions

In the annals of Ethiopian history, a pivotal chapter unfolds with the arrival of European powers on the shores of the Horn of Africa. The Portuguese Connection, marked by early interactions between Ethiopia and European explorers, traders, and missionaries, left an indelible imprint on the cultural, political, and religious landscape of the region.

The 15th and 16th centuries witnessed a surge in European maritime exploration, driven by the desire to establish new trade routes and expand colonial territories. The Portuguese, under the leadership of explorers such as Vasco da Gama, set their sights on the Indian Ocean and the treasures of the East. These maritime endeavors eventually led them to the shores of the Red Sea and the Horn of Africa.

Ethiopia's strategic location as a crossroads of trade and its historical ties to the ancient world made it an attractive destination for European explorers. Portuguese navigators, driven by their ambition to secure trading partners and spread Christianity, sought to establish diplomatic and commercial ties with the Ethiopian rulers.

One of the most notable figures in this early interaction was Portuguese explorer Pêro da Covilhã, who arrived in Ethiopia in the late 15th century. Covilhã's mission was to establish diplomatic and trade connections between Ethiopia and Portugal. His journey, filled with challenges and diplomatic intricacies, marked the beginning of the Portuguese Connection and set the stage for future interactions.

The Portuguese missionaries also played a significant role in the early European engagement with Ethiopia. The Jesuit Order, known for its fervent missionary zeal, sought to spread Christianity in the region and establish a presence within the Ethiopian Orthodox Church. Their efforts were met with mixed reactions, as they encountered resistance from both local religious leaders and Ethiopian rulers.

One of the most notable episodes in the Portuguese Connection was the arrival of Jesuit missionaries in the 16th century, most famously represented by Father Pedro Páez. Páez's linguistic skills and cultural adaptability enabled him to establish rapport with Ethiopian leaders, earning him the favor of Emperor Susenyos. His efforts not only had a profound impact on the spread of Christianity but also on Ethiopia's cultural exchange with Europe.

The Portuguese Connection also had geopolitical implications, as it coincided with regional rivalries and shifting power dynamics. The Portuguese sought to establish themselves as allies against the Ottoman Empire, which was expanding its influence in the Red Sea region. The presence of European powers in the Horn of Africa further complicated the complex interplay of interests among local rulers.

The Portuguese Connection, while marked by cooperation and cultural exchange, was not without its challenges. The differing religious practices, cultural norms, and political agendas often led to misunderstandings and conflicts between the European explorers and the Ethiopian rulers.

Additionally, the influence of the Portuguese missionaries on Ethiopian religious practices sparked debates and tensions within the Ethiopian Orthodox Church.

The legacy of the Portuguese Connection endures in Ethiopia's historical narrative, religious traditions, and cultural interactions. The early European engagement contributed to a period of heightened awareness of Ethiopia within global contexts and exposed the nation to new ideas, technologies, and influences. The presence of Portuguese missionaries left an indelible mark on Ethiopian Christianity, contributing to theological discussions that continue to shape the nation's religious landscape.

As we explore the Portuguese Connection, we are reminded of the complexities of cross-cultural interactions and the enduring impact of historical encounters. This chapter in Ethiopian history serves as a window into the dynamic interplay between global exploration, regional politics, and the exchange of ideas, and invites us to reflect on the far-reaching consequences of early European engagements with the vibrant civilizations of the Horn of Africa.

Emperor Tewodros II: Clash with the British Empire

The mid-19th century marked a tumultuous period in Ethiopian history, characterized by the reign of Emperor Tewodros II, a figure whose ambitions, clashes with foreign powers, and legacy continue to shape the nation's historical narrative. Tewodros' rule, though brief, was marked by a determination to modernize Ethiopia, assert its sovereignty, and navigate a complex web of international relations.

Emperor Tewodros II, born Kassa Haile Giorgis, ascended to the throne in 1855, amidst a backdrop of political fragmentation and external pressures. His reign was defined by a vision to strengthen Ethiopia's centralized authority, unify its diverse regions, and challenge the perceived encroachments of foreign powers.

Tewodros' efforts to modernize Ethiopia's institutions and military capabilities were emblematic of his ambitions to strengthen the nation's sovereignty. He recognized the importance of modern weaponry and European-style organization in maintaining Ethiopia's independence. His attempts to create a centralized state included the establishment of a capital at Magdala and the introduction of European advisors to modernize the country's administrative and military structures.

Tewodros' approach to foreign relations was marked by a blend of pragmatism and defiance. His interactions with European powers, particularly Britain, would come to define his legacy. Seeking political recognition and alliances, Tewodros initiated correspondence with Queen Victoria, expressing his desire for friendship and diplomatic ties. However, his letters went unanswered, setting the stage for a dramatic clash with the British Empire.

The incident that would lead to a confrontation with the British Empire revolved around the British missionary and consul, Captain Charles Cameron. Cameron's imprisonment by Tewodros, ostensibly to secure diplomatic relations, triggered a sequence of events that would culminate in a military expedition led by the British.

The British military expedition to Ethiopia, known as the Abyssinian Expedition, aimed to secure the release of Captain Cameron and other European hostages. Led by Sir Robert Napier, the British forces embarked on a perilous journey to Magdala, facing logistical challenges and treacherous terrain. The conflict that ensued, known as the Battle of Magdala, resulted in the British storming Tewodros' stronghold and capturing the Emperor himself.

The capture of Emperor Tewodros and the fall of Magdala marked a turning point in Ethiopian history. Tewodros chose to take his own life rather than be taken prisoner, a decision that underscored his defiance in the face of foreign intervention. The British forces looted Magdala, seizing artifacts that would later become the center of discussions over repatriation.

The clash between Emperor Tewodros II and the British Empire left a complex legacy. It demonstrated the vulnerabilities of Ethiopia in the face of European imperialism and the challenges of navigating international relations during a period of global power dynamics. Tewodros' resistance to foreign interference symbolized his commitment to Ethiopian sovereignty and his determination to maintain the nation's independence.

The events surrounding Tewodros' reign continue to be the subject of scholarly inquiry, artistic interpretation, and cultural memory. His legacy raises questions about the complexities of modernization, the interplay between tradition and change, and the enduring significance of Ethiopia's interactions with foreign powers. Emperor Tewodros II's clash with the British Empire serves as a poignant reminder of the struggles and choices faced by leaders striving to safeguard their nation's identity, dignity, and autonomy in the face of global challenges.

Abyssinia and Scramble for Africa: Surviving Colonial Intrigues

The late 19th century witnessed a pivotal era in world history known as the Scramble for Africa, a period when European powers vied for control and influence over the vast African continent. Within this intricate geopolitical landscape, Abyssinia, known as Ethiopia, stood as a unique entity that successfully navigated the treacherous waters of colonial ambitions, preserving its independence and cultural identity amidst external pressures.

The Scramble for Africa was driven by European powers' quest for resources, territories, and spheres of influence. As imperial ambitions intensified, Africa became a battleground for competing interests, with colonial powers carving up the continent into territories under their control. However, Ethiopia's position as a sovereign nation with a rich history and resilient institutions set it apart from the fate of many African nations.

Emperor Menelik II, who ruled Ethiopia from 1889 to 1913, played a central role in safeguarding the nation's sovereignty during this tumultuous period. Menelik II recognized the need to modernize Ethiopia's military capabilities to counter external threats. His efforts included procuring modern weaponry and forming alliances with foreign powers, skillfully playing off European rivalries to his advantage.

One of the most pivotal events in Abyssinia's resistance against colonial intrusions was the Battle of Adwa in 1896.

Facing an Italian invasion, Emperor Menelik II led his forces to victory against the European colonial power, marking the first time an African nation decisively defeated a European power in battle during the Scramble for Africa. The victory at Adwa not only solidified Ethiopia's independence but also resonated as a symbol of African resistance against colonialism.

Emperor Menelik II's reign was marked by his efforts to balance modernization with preserving Ethiopia's cultural identity. While adopting certain European administrative practices and technologies, he also championed the nation's traditions and heritage. Menelik II's approach reflected a keen understanding of the complexities of navigating colonial intrigues without compromising Ethiopia's sovereignty.

However, the Scramble for Africa did have some impact on Ethiopia. The nation faced pressures from colonial powers seeking to establish spheres of influence in the region. The Ethiopian Empire signed treaties with European powers to define its boundaries and maintain its autonomy, even as it grappled with external encroachments. The aftermath of these negotiations left Ethiopia with territorial adjustments but maintained its core sovereignty.

The survival of Abyssinia's independence during the Scramble for Africa was not without challenges. European powers continued to engage with Ethiopia diplomatically and attempted to exert influence through economic ties and treaties. Nevertheless, the nation's resilience, its diplomatic acumen, and its internal unity helped it withstand external pressures and maintain its unique identity in the face of global power dynamics.

Abyssinia's ability to navigate the Scramble for Africa with its sovereignty intact resonates as a story of determination, strategic thinking, and the preservation of cultural heritage. Emperor Menelik II's legacy remains one of leadership during a period of uncertainty, demonstrating that even in the face of formidable colonial powers, a nation's identity, history, and collective will can serve as bulwarks against the tide of imperial ambitions. The story of Abyssinia's survival amidst the colonial intrigues of the Scramble for Africa serves as an enduring testament to the power of resilience and the complexities of navigating the geopolitical challenges of a rapidly changing world.

Italian-Ethiopian War: Defiance and Struggle for Sovereignty

The Italian-Ethiopian War of 1935-1936 stands as a pivotal moment in Ethiopian history, marked by a resolute struggle for sovereignty against colonial aggression. This conflict, which pitted the Ethiopian Empire against Fascist Italy, underscored Ethiopia's determination to defend its independence and resist external domination, while revealing the complexities of navigating the global geopolitical landscape of the 20th century.

The roots of the conflict trace back to the imperial ambitions of Fascist Italy under the leadership of Benito Mussolini. Seeking to expand its colonial holdings and avenge a past defeat, Italy set its sights on Ethiopia, which remained one of the few independent African nations. Ethiopia, under the rule of Emperor Haile Selassie I, had successfully navigated the Scramble for Africa and maintained its sovereignty.

The Ethiopian-Eritrean border dispute provided a pretext for Italian aggression. Mussolini's regime exploited this conflict to launch a full-scale invasion of Ethiopia in 1935. The Italian forces, equipped with modern weaponry and superior military technology, sought to subdue the Ethiopian Empire within a short span of time.

Emperor Haile Selassie I rallied his nation in the face of this unprecedented threat. His appeal to the League of Nations in defense of Ethiopia's sovereignty was met with limited international support, highlighting the challenges of rallying the global community against colonial ambitions. Despite the odds, the Ethiopian resistance was fueled by a deep sense of national pride, a fervent commitment to independence, and a determination to repel the invaders.

The Ethiopian forces, though outnumbered and outgunned, displayed remarkable courage and ingenuity on the battlefield. They employed guerilla tactics, utilized the challenging terrain to their advantage, and showcased their resilience in the face of adversity. The Battle of Adwa's legacy loomed large, serving as a source of inspiration and a reminder of Ethiopia's history of successful resistance against foreign aggression.

The conflict also revealed the limitations of the League of Nations and the international community's ability to prevent the violation of a nation's sovereignty. While some nations imposed economic sanctions on Italy, these measures fell short of halting the Italian aggression. This failure to effectively counter colonial ambitions underscored the challenges of enforcing collective security in a world marked by power politics and competing interests.

Despite the Ethiopian resistance, the Italian forces eventually occupied the capital city of Addis Ababa in 1936. Emperor Haile Selassie I was forced into exile, and Italy formally established the colony of Italian East Africa, comprising Ethiopia, Eritrea, and Italian Somaliland. The occupation of Ethiopia was met with international condemnation, but the global response was insufficient to reverse the course of events.

Ethiopia's occupation was short-lived, as the outbreak of World War II shifted the dynamics of power. As British and Allied forces advanced in North Africa, Italy's hold on Ethiopia weakened. In 1941, British and Ethiopian forces, with the support of local resistance movements, liberated the nation from Italian occupation, restoring Emperor Haile Selassie I to the throne.

The Italian-Ethiopian War is a testament to the resilience of a nation in the face of aggression, the complexities of international diplomacy, and the global struggles for sovereignty that defined the 20th century. The Ethiopian resistance against Italy's colonial ambitions stands as an enduring symbol of the nation's commitment to its identity, heritage, and the preservation of its independence in the face of formidable challenges.

Haile Selassie: The Lion of Judah's Reign and Legacy

Emperor Haile Selassie I, whose given name was Ras Tafari Makonnen, stands as one of the most iconic figures in Ethiopian history, leaving an indelible mark on the nation's trajectory during a period of immense change and global challenges. Haile Selassie's reign, spanning from 1930 to 1974, encompassed moments of triumph, resilience, and complex interactions with the international community.

Born in 1892 to noble lineage, Haile Selassie's ascent to the throne was marked by his selection as Regent in 1916 and later as Emperor in 1930, following the death of Empress Zewditu. His coronation marked a significant turning point in Ethiopian history, as he became the 225th monarch in a lineage believed to be descended from King Solomon and the Queen of Sheba, known as the Solomonic Dynasty.

Haile Selassie's reign was characterized by his commitment to modernization, reform, and preserving Ethiopia's sovereignty. Recognizing the need to adapt to changing global dynamics, he initiated a series of reforms aimed at modernizing Ethiopia's institutions, economy, and infrastructure. These efforts included the introduction of a constitution, educational reforms, and the construction of roads, hospitals, and schools.

The Emperor's engagement with the international community was marked by his pursuit of diplomatic relations, efforts to gain recognition for Ethiopia, and his role as a spokesperson for the broader African continent. He sought to navigate the challenges of a world in the midst of upheaval, including the aftermath of World War II and the decolonization movement that swept across Africa.

One of the most iconic moments in Haile Selassie's legacy was his address to the League of Nations in 1936, following the Italian invasion. His impassioned plea for collective security and defense of Ethiopia's sovereignty resonated globally, and his speech served as a powerful reminder of the importance of international cooperation in the face of aggression.

Haile Selassie's reign was not without its internal challenges. The modernization efforts and centralized authority he sought to establish encountered resistance from traditionalists and regional power centers. Additionally, economic disparities and social inequalities persisted, prompting calls for reform and justice from various segments of society.

The Emperor's commitment to Ethiopian Orthodoxy and his status as a spiritual leader held immense significance. He was seen as the earthly representation of the Lion of Judah, a symbol that carried deep spiritual and cultural resonance. Haile Selassie's role within the Ethiopian Orthodox Church, his patronage of religious institutions, and his engagement in matters of faith reinforced his connection to the nation's religious identity.

However, Haile Selassie's reign was not without controversy. Critics point to instances of political repression, limitations on civil liberties, and challenges in addressing the diverse needs of Ethiopia's population. His efforts to balance modernization with preserving tradition were met with varying degrees of success, and debates over his legacy continue to shape discussions about Ethiopia's history.

The Emperor's downfall came in 1974, as internal discontent, economic challenges, and calls for political change culminated in a military coup that marked the end of the Solomonic Dynasty's rule. Haile Selassie was deposed and imprisoned, and he passed away in 1975 under unclear circumstances.

Haile Selassie's legacy endures as a complex tapestry of triumphs, challenges, and enduring symbolism. His reign reflects the complexities of modernization, diplomacy, and nation-building in the midst of global transformation. His status as a cultural and spiritual icon, particularly within the Rastafari movement, has extended his influence beyond Ethiopia's borders, making him a figure of international significance. Haile Selassie's reign and legacy remind us of the intricate interplay between leadership, tradition, modernity, and the enduring power of symbolism in shaping a nation's identity and historical narrative.

Ethiopia's Struggle for Liberation: From Occupation to Independence

The years following World War II witnessed Ethiopia's determined struggle for liberation, as the nation sought to cast off the shackles of occupation and reaffirm its sovereignty. This period, marked by resilience, resistance, and diplomatic maneuvering, reflects the complexities of navigating global dynamics and asserting a nation's right to self-determination.

The aftermath of World War II brought shifts in global power dynamics, leading to renewed efforts towards decolonization and the restoration of independent states. Ethiopia, which had faced Italian occupation during the 1930s and early 1940s, found itself at the crossroads of these geopolitical changes.

The return of Emperor Haile Selassie I to Ethiopia in 1941, following the liberation from Italian occupation, marked a symbolic moment of national renewal. The Emperor's presence served as a rallying point for the nation's aspirations and a testament to the resilience of the Ethiopian people in the face of external aggression.

The post-war period saw Ethiopia's engagement with the international community in pursuit of recognition and support for its quest for independence. Emperor Haile Selassie I played a pivotal role in advocating for Ethiopia's interests on the global stage. His participation in the establishment of the United Nations and his diplomatic efforts resonated with the principles of sovereignty and self-determination enshrined in international law.

Ethiopia's struggle for liberation was not limited to diplomatic endeavors. The Emperor's commitment to modernization continued, as he initiated a series of reforms aimed at strengthening the nation's institutions, economy, and social fabric. These reforms were intended to address longstanding challenges and pave the way for a more inclusive and prosperous Ethiopia.

However, the path to independence was not without challenges. The question of Eritrea's status within Ethiopia emerged as a contentious issue. Eritrea had been under British administration following Italy's defeat, and discussions about its future led to a series of negotiations and debates. Ultimately, in 1952, the United Nations decided to federate Eritrea with Ethiopia, leading to tensions and later conflict.

The 1950s and 1960s saw a wave of decolonization across Africa, as nations gained independence from colonial powers. Ethiopia's trajectory was influenced by these global shifts, as well as its unique historical context. The Emperor's efforts to modernize the nation, while preserving its cultural heritage, served as a model for other African states seeking to forge their paths to independence.

The internal dynamics of Ethiopia's struggle for liberation were influenced by regional and ethnic diversity. Various regions within Ethiopia sought to assert their identities and rights within the framework of a unified nation. These dynamics contributed to discussions about federalism, regional autonomy, and the role of the central government in a changing landscape.

Ethiopia's diplomatic efforts culminated in its successful defense against foreign intervention. The conflict over Eritrea's status escalated into a war with neighboring powers, testing Ethiopia's military capabilities and national unity. However, Ethiopia's resilience and determination enabled it to retain control over its sovereignty and territorial integrity.

In 1974, Ethiopia's struggle for liberation took a new turn with the fall of Emperor Haile Selassie I. The military coup that deposed the Emperor and established a Marxist-Leninist regime known as the Derg marked a new chapter in the nation's history. The struggle for liberation took on new dimensions, as Ethiopians sought to navigate the challenges of internal governance, human rights, and political stability.

The chapter of Ethiopia's struggle for liberation, from occupation to independence, reflects the complexities of forging a national identity amidst global transformations. It highlights the nation's resilience, its engagement with international institutions, and the delicate balance between modernization and preserving tradition. Ethiopia's path to independence serves as a testament to the enduring power of a nation's will to assert its sovereignty, shape its destiny, and navigate the intricacies of a rapidly changing world.

Derg Regime: Marxism, Mengistu, and Massacre

The Derg regime, a Marxist-Leninist government that ruled Ethiopia from 1974 to 1991, stands as a dark and tumultuous chapter in the nation's history. This period, marked by political repression, economic hardship, and widespread human rights abuses, reflects the complexities of attempting to transform a nation's socio-political landscape through radical ideologies and centralized control.

The Derg regime emerged from the ashes of the military coup that deposed Emperor Haile Selassie I in 1974. Led by a group of military officers, the Derg promised to address the nation's grievances and implement radical reforms aimed at creating a more equitable society. The regime's leadership, with Mengistu Haile Mariam at its helm, aimed to establish a Marxist-Leninist state characterized by state ownership of industries, land redistribution, and collectivization.

The regime's pursuit of Marxism-Leninism was met with mixed reactions. While some segments of society supported the promise of socio-economic transformation, others were wary of the regime's tactics and the potential for political repression. The Derg's rhetoric of class struggle and anti-imperialism resonated with a portion of the population, but its implementation led to a centralized and authoritarian government.

Mengistu Haile Mariam's leadership of the Derg marked a period of brutal rule. The regime sought to quell dissent through violent means, leading to a series of purges, arrests, and executions of perceived opponents. The Red Terror campaign, launched in the late 1970s, resulted in the deaths of tens of thousands of Ethiopians, with many more subjected to torture and imprisonment.

Economically, the Derg's policies had mixed results. The regime's efforts to nationalize industries and redistribute land were intended to address inequalities, but they also disrupted established economic systems and led to agricultural inefficiencies. The imposition of collectivization and forced resettlement programs further exacerbated economic challenges, leading to food shortages and famine.

Ethiopia's international relations during the Derg regime were marked by shifting allegiances. While the regime initially aligned itself with the Soviet Union, it later sought aid and support from various countries, including the United States. The geopolitics of the Cold War era influenced the nation's diplomatic strategies and its role within the global community.

The Derg regime's actions had devastating consequences for Ethiopia's diverse population. Ethnic tensions were exacerbated by the regime's policies, and various regions within the country sought to assert their identities and autonomy. These tensions escalated into armed conflicts, notably in Eritrea and Tigray, where groups sought self-determination and an end to the regime's oppressive rule.

The international community's response to the Derg regime was complex. While some nations provided support or diplomatic recognition, others condemned the regime's human rights abuses and its disregard for democratic principles. Humanitarian efforts to address the famine of the 1980s highlighted the plight of the Ethiopian people and the dire consequences of the regime's policies.

The downfall of the Derg regime came in 1991, as a coalition of rebel groups known as the Ethiopian People's Revolutionary Democratic Front (EPRDF) overthrew the government. Mengistu Haile Mariam fled into exile, and the Derg's rule officially ended. The legacy of the regime's actions, however, continues to shape Ethiopia's trajectory and national identity.

The Derg regime's legacy is marked by the lasting scars of political repression, economic upheaval, and human rights abuses. Its radical ideological agenda clashed with the realities of governance, leading to a tragic period of turmoil for the Ethiopian people. The chapter of the Derg regime serves as a stark reminder of the complexities of attempting to reshape a nation's destiny through authoritarian means, and underscores the enduring struggle for freedom, justice, and dignity in the face of oppressive rule.

Eritrean Independence: Birth of a New Nation

The journey towards Eritrean independence stands as a testament to the aspirations, struggles, and sacrifices of a people determined to chart their own destiny. This chapter in Ethiopian history reflects the complexities of identity, colonial legacies, and the pursuit of self-determination within the context of a changing global landscape.

Eritrea's historical trajectory was marked by a complex blend of cultural, ethnic, and religious diversity. The region's strategic location along the Red Sea had drawn the attention of various powers throughout history, including the Ottoman Empire and Italy. Eritrea's colonial experience under Italian rule during the late 19th and early 20th centuries deeply influenced its modern political consciousness.

The end of World War II brought the Eritrean question to the forefront of international discussions. Eritrea's future status became a subject of negotiation, with various parties proposing different paths, including integration with Ethiopia, an autonomous entity within a federation, or full independence. The United Nations entered the fray, and Eritrea's fate hung in the balance.

In 1952, the United Nations decided to federate Eritrea with Ethiopia, a decision that sparked resistance and discord within the Eritrean population. While some groups welcomed the federation as an opportunity for mutual development, others viewed it as a continuation of colonial subjugation. This discord set the stage for a struggle that would culminate in Eritrea's quest for independence.

The 1960s witnessed a resurgence of Eritrean nationalism, fueled by discontent with the Ethiopian central government's policies and demands for greater autonomy. The Eritrean Liberation Front (ELF) emerged as a key player in the struggle, seeking self-determination and an end to what many perceived as Ethiopian oppression. Armed conflict erupted, with Eritrean fighters clashing with Ethiopian forces.

The landscape of Eritrean resistance shifted with the emergence of the Eritrean People's Liberation Front (EPLF) in the 1970s. Led by Isaias Afwerki, the EPLF adopted a more centralized and disciplined approach to armed struggle, effectively gaining control over large swathes of Eritrean territory. The EPLF's ability to provide social services, administer justice, and build a parallel state structure contributed to its growing support.

The overthrow of Ethiopia's Derg regime in 1991 marked a turning point. The EPLF, alongside other Ethiopian rebel groups, toppled the Derg and paved the way for Eritrean independence. In 1993, after a referendum that saw an overwhelming majority vote in favor of independence, Eritrea officially became a sovereign nation.

Eritrea's independence was met with hope and optimism, as well as the challenges of nation-building. The process of forging a cohesive national identity, addressing the scars of conflict, and building political and economic institutions presented formidable tasks. Eritrea's diverse population, which included various ethnic and religious groups, added complexity to the process.

However, Eritrea's post-independence trajectory also encountered challenges. The new nation struggled to establish democratic governance, manage its economy, and navigate regional dynamics. The border dispute with Ethiopia, which flared into a full-scale war between 1998 and 2000, underscored the complexities of post-independence nation-building and the fragility of regional stability.

Eritrea's internal dynamics have also been influenced by political repression and restrictions on civil liberties. The nation's focus on security and stability has at times led to tensions with international actors and human rights organizations. Eritrea's complex relationship with the global community and its policies have been subject to scrutiny and debate.

Eritrea's journey towards independence reflects the enduring power of self-determination and the complexities of navigating a nation's path within the context of historical legacies and shifting global dynamics. The birth of a new nation in Eritrea serves as a reminder of the struggles and triumphs of a people determined to shape their own destiny, and stands as a chapter in Ethiopian history that continues to influence discussions about identity, autonomy, and the pursuit of sovereignty.

Ethiopian People's Revolutionary Democratic Front (EPRDF): Winds of Change

The Ethiopian People's Revolutionary Democratic Front (EPRDF) emerged as a transformative force in Ethiopian politics, ushering in a new era of governance, reform, and societal change. This chapter in Ethiopian history reflects the complexities of transitioning from authoritarian rule to a multi-ethnic federal system, as well as the challenges and achievements that accompanied this period of transition.

The EPRDF was founded in 1989 as a coalition of rebel groups that had played a crucial role in overthrowing the Derg regime. Comprising ethnic-based factions, including the Tigray People's Liberation Front (TPLF) and the Oromo Liberation Front (OLF), the EPRDF sought to address the nation's diverse identities and aspirations through a decentralized federal framework.

The EPRDF's rise to power was marked by a series of military victories against the Derg regime, culminating in the capture of Addis Ababa in 1991. This event signaled the end of decades of authoritarian rule and marked the beginning of a new political trajectory for Ethiopia. The EPRDF's leaders, notably Meles Zenawi, took on the task of governing a nation marked by ethnic diversity, regional disparities, and a legacy of conflict.

The establishment of a federal system marked a departure from Ethiopia's previous centralized governance model. The EPRDF's approach aimed to devolve power to regional states based on ethnic lines, granting them a degree of autonomy in matters such as culture, language, and administration. This federal structure was intended to address the historical grievances of different ethnic groups and promote inclusivity.

Economic reform was also a cornerstone of the EPRDF's agenda. The regime implemented policies aimed at modernizing agriculture, promoting investment, and improving infrastructure. The liberalization of key sectors, such as telecommunications, aimed to attract foreign investment and spur economic growth. However, the pace and outcomes of these reforms varied, and challenges persisted in addressing poverty and inequality.

The EPRDF's governance model emphasized ethnic representation and participation in decision-making processes. While this approach aimed to empower previously marginalized groups, it also raised questions about the balance between ethnic identity and national unity. The emphasis on ethnicity sometimes resulted in tensions between regions and contributed to debates about the nature of Ethiopian identity.

Ethiopia's engagement with the international community evolved under the EPRDF. The regime sought foreign assistance and partnerships, while also positioning itself as a regional leader. Ethiopia's role in peacekeeping missions, diplomatic negotiations, and initiatives such as the African Union demonstrated its ambitions to play a constructive role on the global stage.

The EPRDF's tenure was not without challenges and controversies. Tensions between ethnic groups flared at times, and questions about political freedoms and human rights emerged. The 2005 elections highlighted these tensions, as disputes over the results led to violence and arrests. The

EPRDF's response underscored the complexities of managing a diverse society during a period of democratic transition.

Meles Zenawi's passing in 2012 marked a significant turning point for the EPRDF. His leadership had shaped Ethiòpia's post-Derg trajectory, and his absence raised questions about the EPRDF's future direction. The transition of power within the party and the appointment of Hailemariam Desalegn as Prime Minister marked a phase of continued governance, reform, and evolving challenges.

Ethiopia's path under the EPRDF saw progress, but it also underscored the intricate balance between governance, identity, and development. The regime's emphasis on ethnic representation, federalism, and economic growth marked a departure from Ethiopia's past, but challenges persisted in navigating the complexities of diversity and promoting equitable development.

The EPRDF's legacy continues to shape Ethiopia's trajectory. The party's tenure ultimately ended in 2018, as public protests and demands for change led to the appointment of Abiy Ahmed as Prime Minister. Abiy's tenure ushered in a period of political reform, regional reconciliation, and discussions about Ethiopia's future direction.

The EPRDF's journey through Ethiopia's political landscape reflects the complexities of governance, diversity, and reform. The winds of change brought by the EPRDF altered the course of Ethiopian history, leaving an enduring impact on discussions about governance, identity, and the pursuit of development. The chapter of the EPRDF's rule serves as a reminder of the complexities of transitioning from authoritarianism to democracy and the challenges of steering a nation towards inclusive growth and unity.

Ethiopian-Eritrean Conflict: Unraveling and Reconciliation

The Ethiopian-Eritrean conflict, which spanned decades and led to a devastating war, stands as a complex tale of identity, territorial disputes, and geopolitical intricacies. This chapter in Ethiopian history reflects the challenges of maintaining stability in a region marked by historical legacies, political ambitions, and the quest for self-determination.

The roots of the conflict trace back to Eritrea's historical trajectory within the Ethiopian empire. Following Italy's defeat in World War II, Eritrea was under British administration and later federated with Ethiopia in 1952. The decision to federate Eritrea within Ethiopia led to tensions and resistance, as Eritrean nationalist movements sought independence.

The Ethiopian Revolution of 1974 and the subsequent fall of Emperor Haile Selassie I marked a turning point in the relationship between Ethiopia and Eritrea. The revolutionary government's efforts to address ethnic and regional disparities contributed to calls for greater autonomy and self-determination within Eritrea. The struggle for independence gained momentum as Eritrean rebel groups, notably the Eritrean People's Liberation Front (EPLF), waged a protracted armed struggle.

Eritrea's quest for independence culminated in 1991, as the EPRDF-led forces overthrew the Ethiopian Derg regime. Eritrea held a referendum in 1993, resulting in an overwhelming vote in favor of independence. Eritrea emerged as a sovereign nation, marking a historic moment in the pursuit of self-determination.

However, the euphoria of Eritrea's independence was short-lived. Disputes over the demarcation of the border between Ethiopia and Eritrea, particularly in the town of Badme, quickly escalated into a full-scale war in 1998. The conflict, characterized by fierce battles and devastating human loss, brought the region to the brink of catastrophe.

The war's consequences were severe, with both nations enduring economic hardships, displacement, and loss of life. International efforts to mediate the conflict, led by the Algiers Agreement, yielded a peace agreement in 2000 that established a ceasefire and a boundary commission to resolve the border dispute. However, disagreements over the implementation of the commission's decisions hindered progress towards lasting peace.

The Ethiopian-Eritrean conflict had broader regional implications, influencing diplomatic relations and alliances in the Horn of Africa. Both nations sought to exert influence over neighboring countries, and the conflict's ramifications were felt beyond their borders. The dynamics of the conflict also intersected with global power dynamics and international interests, shaping the responses of external actors.

A significant breakthrough in the conflict's resolution came in 2018, with the appointment of Abiy Ahmed as Prime Minister of Ethiopia. Abiy's administration embarked on a policy of reconciliation and cooperation with Eritrea, marking a dramatic departure from the previous status quo. In a historic moment, Abiy and Eritrean President Isaias

Afwerki signed the Joint Declaration of Peace and Friendship in 2018, effectively ending the state of war and reestablishing diplomatic relations.

The reconciliation efforts between Ethiopia and Eritrea led to the reopening of borders, the resumption of flights, and a thawing of relations. The conflict's end brought hope for stability and cooperation in a region marked by decades of tension. However, the process of healing and addressing the wounds of the conflict remained complex, as both nations navigated the challenges of reconciliation, trust-building, and addressing the needs of their citizens.

The Ethiopian-Eritrean conflict, its unraveling, and subsequent reconciliation serve as a poignant reminder of the human cost of territorial disputes and geopolitical rivalries. The journey from war to peace underscores the complexities of conflict resolution, the power of visionary leadership, and the enduring quest for stability in a region marked by shared history and interconnected destinies. This chapter in Ethiopian history stands as a testament to the possibilities of healing and collaboration, even in the face of longstanding enmities and historical grievances.

Ancient Script and Language: Unveiling Ge'ez and Amharic

The rich tapestry of Ethiopia's linguistic and written heritage is intricately woven with the evolution of ancient scripts and languages that have shaped the nation's identity and historical narrative. Among these, Ge'ez and Amharic stand as key pillars, representing centuries of cultural expression, religious devotion, and communication.

The Ge'ez Script and Language:

The Ge'ez script, also known as Ethiopic, has its origins deeply rooted in ancient Ethiopia. It is one of the oldest writing systems in the world, with its earliest inscriptions dating back to the 5th century AD. Ge'ez has played a central role in Ethiopia's cultural and religious life, particularly within the Ethiopian Orthodox Church.

Ge'ez is a syllabic script characterized by a unique combination of consonants and vowels. The script has evolved over time, with various forms and styles reflecting different historical periods. Ge'ez was traditionally written on parchment or papyrus, and it was used for religious texts, historical records, and literary works.

The Ge'ez language, closely associated with the script, is a Semitic language that has left a profound impact on Ethiopia's linguistic landscape. It served as a liturgical language for the Ethiopian Orthodox Church and contributed to the development of Amharic and other Ethiopian languages. Ge'ez's enduring influence is evident in the preservation of religious manuscripts, hymns, and theological works.

The Emergence of Amharic:

Amharic, Ethiopia's official language, has its roots in the Ge'ez language but developed into a distinct and vibrant language over time. Amharic's rise to prominence can be attributed to its use by various Ethiopian dynasties, the growth of trade and commerce, and its widespread adoption as a lingua franca among diverse ethnic groups.

Amharic's script evolved from the Ge'ez script, with modifications to accommodate its phonetic structure and linguistic nuances. The script's flexibility and adaptability contributed to Amharic's popularity as a written language for both secular and religious purposes. Amharic manuscripts, historical records, poetry, and literature showcase the depth and richness of the language.

Amharic's significance extends beyond communication—it is an integral part of Ethiopia's cultural identity. It is the medium through which oral traditions, folklore, historical narratives, and contemporary discourse are expressed. The Amharic language has facilitated the exchange of ideas, the preservation of history, and the articulation of the Ethiopian experience.

Cultural and Religious Significance:

Both Ge'ez and Amharic have profound cultural and religious significance. Ge'ez, as the language of religious texts, liturgical chants, and ancient manuscripts, is integral to the Ethiopian Orthodox Church's worship and spirituality. It serves as a bridge between past and present, connecting contemporary worshippers with centuries of tradition.

Amharic's role in Ethiopian culture is equally significant. It has been instrumental in transmitting Ethiopia's diverse cultural heritage through literature, poetry, and storytelling. The works of renowned Ethiopian poets and writers, such as Tsegaye Gabre-Medhin and Haddis Alemayehu, have helped shape Amharic as a language of literary expression and artistic creativity.

Continued Legacy and Modern Usage:

Today, Ge'ez and Amharic continue to thrive in Ethiopia's linguistic landscape. While Ge'ez remains primarily a liturgical language, Amharic is the medium through which education, media, administration, and daily communication unfold. The establishment of modern Amharic literature, newspapers, and digital media has further expanded its reach and influence.

The journey of these ancient scripts and languages reflects Ethiopia's enduring commitment to preserving its cultural heritage and fostering linguistic diversity. Ge'ez and Amharic stand as testament to the profound ways in which language shapes identity, connects generations, and serves as a vessel for knowledge, expression, and collective memory. Through these linguistic treasures, Ethiopia's past and present converge, creating a narrative thread that weaves together centuries of tradition and innovation.

Coptic Christianity: Spiritual Pillar of Ethiopian Identity

Coptic Christianity, deeply intertwined with Ethiopia's history, culture, and identity, has been a spiritual cornerstone that has shaped the nation's ethos and way of life. From the earliest days of its introduction to the present, Coptic Christianity has played a pivotal role in Ethiopian society, fostering a unique fusion of faith, tradition, and heritage.

Origins and Early Influence:

Coptic Christianity was introduced to Ethiopia in the 4th century, marking a significant turning point in the nation's religious landscape. The roots of this faith can be traced back to Egypt, where it flourished as an early Christian tradition. Christianity's arrival in Ethiopia was closely tied to the legendary story of the Ethiopian eunuch's conversion by Philip the Evangelist, as recounted in the New Testament's Book of Acts.

The Ethiopian Orthodox Tewahedo Church, an ancient and independent Christian denomination, became the spiritual home for Coptic Christianity in Ethiopia. The term "Tewahedo" signifies the church's belief in the unity of Christ's divine and human natures, a doctrine that set it apart from other Christian traditions.

Spiritual and Liturgical Traditions:

Coptic Christianity brought with it a rich tapestry of spiritual and liturgical traditions that have profoundly shaped Ethiopian religious practice. The liturgy of the Ethiopian Orthodox Church is characterized by its solemnity, intricate rituals, and use of ancient languages such as Ge'ez. Liturgical chants, hymns, and iconography are integral components of worship, creating a deeply immersive and contemplative experience.

Monasticism, an essential aspect of Coptic Christianity, also took root in Ethiopia. Monasteries, often situated in remote and serene landscapes, became centers of spiritual devotion, theological learning, and cultural preservation. These monastic communities continue to maintain ascetic practices, maintain ancient manuscripts, and serve as custodians of the church's heritage.

Coptic Christianity and Ethiopian Identity:

Coptic Christianity has played a significant role in shaping Ethiopian identity. It provided a spiritual framework through which the nation's historical narratives, cultural values, and communal solidarity were expressed. The Ethiopian Orthodox Church's teachings and rituals have permeated all aspects of life, from birth to death, and have guided Ethiopians through triumphs and tribulations.

The church's emphasis on social justice, compassion, and community welfare has resonated deeply within Ethiopian society. Its teachings have influenced governance, ethics, and cultural norms, shaping the moral compass of the nation. The church's role as a source of guidance, solace, and unity has remained steadfast throughout Ethiopia's history.

Ethiopian Saints and Hagiography:

Coptic Christianity's influence is also evident in the veneration of Ethiopian saints and the tradition of hagiography. Ethiopian hagiographical texts celebrate the lives of saints such as Abbo, Tekle Haymanot, and Aregawi, highlighting their spiritual achievements, miracles, and contributions to the church. These narratives have helped forge a link between the faithful and their spiritual forebears, fostering a sense of continuity and shared devotion.

Challenges and Resilience:

Throughout its history, Coptic Christianity in Ethiopia faced challenges from both external forces and internal dynamics. Islamic expansions in neighboring regions led to periods of conflict and upheaval. Additionally, the church navigated challenges arising from political changes and the pressures of modernization. However, Coptic Christianity's resilience is evident in its ability to adapt, preserve its core beliefs, and maintain its spiritual relevance.

Contemporary Relevance:

In contemporary Ethiopia, Coptic Christianity maintains its significance. The Ethiopian Orthodox Church continues to be a central institution in the lives of millions of Ethiopians. The church's influence extends beyond spiritual matters to education, healthcare, and social services. It remains a unifying force, transcending ethnic, linguistic, and regional divisions.

Coptic Christianity's enduring legacy speaks to its ability to transcend time and space. It has not only fostered spiritual growth but has also served as a catalyst for preserving Ethiopia's cultural heritage, promoting social cohesion, and nourishing the nation's soul. Through its teachings, rituals, and values, Coptic Christianity remains an indelible spiritual pillar that continues to shape Ethiopian identity and inspire generations to come.

Timket Festival: Celebration of Epiphany and Faith

The Timket Festival, a vibrant and revered event in Ethiopian culture, is a celebration that illuminates the nation with its spiritual significance, communal joy, and cultural vibrancy. This chapter delves into the essence of Timket, capturing its history, rituals, and enduring resonance as a testament to Ethiopian faith and identity.

Roots in Epiphany:

Timket, also known as Epiphany, derives its name from the Greek word "Theophany," meaning the manifestation of God. The festival commemorates the baptism of Jesus Christ in the Jordan River by John the Baptist, a pivotal event symbolizing Christ's revelation as the Son of God.

Spiritual Pilgrimage:

Timket unfolds in various stages, with each stage contributing to the festival's profound spiritual significance. The eve of Timket, known as Ketera, involves a solemn procession of the Tabot, a symbolic representation of the Ark of the Covenant, from churches to a central water source. This procession is accompanied by prayers, hymns, and the illumination of bonfires.

The Joyous Celebration:

Timket's main event takes place on the day of Epiphany, when the faithful gather near water bodies, often replicating the Jordan River, for the grand procession and blessing of the waters. This momentous occasion is marked by a colorful display of traditional attire, joyful songs, and vibrant dance. Priests lead the ceremony, and the Tabots are bathed in the water, an act believed to sanctify and bless the water.

Symbolism and Spirituality:

Timket's symbolism is rich and multi-layered. The Tabot's journey echoes Christ's baptism, while the immersion in water signifies spiritual cleansing and renewal. The blessed water is distributed to the participants, who consider it a source of spiritual healing and protection. The communal participation and shared faith bind individuals together in a profound experience of devotion and unity.

Cultural Heritage and Tradition:

Beyond its spiritual significance, Timket is an embodiment of Ethiopia's cultural heritage. The festival is a showcase of traditional clothing, music, and dance. Elaborate costumes, embroidered garments, and vibrant accessories add a kaleidoscope of color to the celebrations. Drumming, ululating, and festive songs accompany the processions, creating an immersive sensory experience.

Regional Variations:

Timket is celebrated across Ethiopia, each region adding its unique cultural flair to the festivities. In Lalibela, home to the famous rock-hewn churches, Timket is an exceptional spectacle, with thousands of pilgrims and visitors converging to witness the ceremonies. In Addis Ababa and other urban centers, Timket is a joyful occasion celebrated by diverse communities.

Spiritual Reflection and Social Bonding:

Timket transcends the religious realm, fostering social cohesion and family bonds. Families and friends gather to partake in the festivities, sharing food, laughter, and prayers. The festival also provides an opportunity for introspection, as individuals reflect on their faith, seek forgiveness, and renew their commitment to spiritual growth.

Continuity and Contemporary Relevance:

In modern times, Timket retains its significance and allure. The festival continues to draw pilgrims, tourists, and Ethiopians alike. Its spiritual depth and cultural richness make it a symbol of Ethiopia's unwavering faith and enduring heritage. Timket also serves as an opportunity for Ethiopia to share its cultural treasures with the world, fostering cross-cultural understanding and appreciation.

Timket's Enduring Light:

The Timket Festival stands as a luminous testament to the fusion of faith, culture, and identity. It carries forward the legacy of Ethiopia's spiritual heritage, embodying the nation's deep-rooted devotion and unity. The celebration of Timket illuminates not only the Ethiopian landscape but also the hearts of those who partake in its rituals, inspiring a profound sense of connectedness, renewal, and reverence.

Simien Mountains: Breathtaking Landscapes and Diverse Wildlife

Nestled in the rugged heart of Ethiopia, the Simien Mountains National Park stands as a breathtaking testament to the natural beauty and ecological diversity that define the region. This chapter unveils the grandeur of the Simien Mountains, exploring its stunning landscapes, unique wildlife, and the delicate balance between conservation and human interaction.

A Geological Masterpiece:

The Simien Mountains are a UNESCO World Heritage Site, and for good reason. This majestic mountain range was shaped millions of years ago by tectonic forces and erosion, resulting in dramatic escarpments, deep valleys, and towering peaks. The highest point, Ras Dashen, stands at an impressive elevation of 4,533 meters (14,872 feet).

Spectacular Landscapes:

The landscapes of the Simien Mountains are a tapestry of contrasts. From the dizzying heights of the escarpments to the lush valleys below, the terrain unfolds in a series of awe-inspiring panoramas. Jagged cliffs, deep canyons, and verdant plateaus form a dynamic tableau that is both humbling and captivating.

Diverse Ecosystems:

The Simien Mountains harbor a diverse range of ecosystems, each uniquely adapted to the rugged terrain and changing altitudes. From the Afroalpine moorlands at the highest elevations to the montane forests and grasslands, the park is a living laboratory of biodiversity. This rich mosaic of habitats supports a wide array of plant and animal species.

Wildlife Sanctuary:

One of the park's most captivating features is its remarkable wildlife. The Simien Mountains are home to unique and often endemic species that have adapted to the challenging environment. The most iconic resident is the Ethiopian wolf, the rarest canid in the world. Other notable species include the walia ibex, an agile mountain goat, and the gelada baboon, recognizable by its impressive "bleeding heart" patch on the chest.

Conservation Challenges:

Despite its natural splendor, the Simien Mountains face challenges that threaten their delicate ecosystem. Human encroachment, agricultural expansion, and the pressures of tourism can disrupt the balance of nature. Conservation efforts strive to strike a harmonious balance between preserving the park's biodiversity and providing sustainable livelihoods for local communities.

Ethiopian Wolf Conservation Program:

The Ethiopian wolf, also known as the "red fox," is a flagship species for conservation in the Simien Mountains.

Efforts to protect and conserve this critically endangered carnivore have led to the establishment of the Ethiopian Wolf Conservation Program. This initiative aims to mitigate human-wolf conflicts, conduct research, and raise awareness about the importance of preserving the species and its habitat.

Trekking and Adventure:

The Simien Mountains offer a paradise for trekking enthusiasts and adventure seekers. The park features a network of well-marked trails that lead intrepid explorers through its diverse landscapes. Treks can range from short day hikes to multi-day expeditions that traverse varying altitudes and offer breathtaking views.

Cultural Encounters:

The Simien Mountains are not only a realm of natural wonders but also a place where visitors can experience the rich cultures of the local communities. The park is inhabited by diverse ethnic groups, including the Amhara, who have maintained a way of life closely connected to the land and its resources.

A Call for Responsible Tourism:

As the allure of the Simien Mountains draws more visitors, the importance of responsible tourism becomes paramount. Efforts are being made to ensure that tourism contributes to the park's conservation and the well-being of local communities. Sustainable practices, respectful interactions with wildlife, and the education of visitors about the park's fragility are all key components of these efforts.

A Living Legacy:

The Simien Mountains are more than a collection of rocks and valleys; they are a living legacy that speaks to the power and beauty of nature. The park's towering peaks, vibrant flora, and unique wildlife remind us of the intricate connections that bind all life on Earth. As we venture into the Simien Mountains, we not only witness nature's grandeur but also affirm our responsibility to protect and cherish the remarkable landscapes that inspire awe and wonder.

Rift Valley Lakes: Ecological Gems and Avian Paradises

Nestled within the dramatic embrace of the East African Rift Valley, a series of sparkling jewels beckons to explorers and nature enthusiasts alike. The Rift Valley Lakes, a cluster of serene bodies of water, are more than mere landmarks—they are ecological gems and avian paradises that reveal the intricate dance of nature in one of the world's most dynamic geological settings.

A Geological Tapestry:

The Rift Valley Lakes are a testament to the Earth's ever-changing landscape. Created by the tectonic forces that have shaped the Great Rift Valley, this interconnected series of lakes stretches across East Africa, encompassing a variety of sizes, depths, and altitudes. Each lake is a chapter in the geological history of the region, contributing to the awe-inspiring diversity of landscapes.

Biodiversity Hotspots:

These lakes are not just bodies of water; they are life-supporting ecosystems that are home to a staggering array of flora and fauna. The lush surroundings, fertile soils, and temperate climates create an environment that sustains an incredible diversity of life. From aquatic plants to thriving fish populations, the Rift Valley Lakes form vital habitats that are teeming with life.

Avian Wonderlands:

One of the most enchanting features of the Rift Valley Lakes is their role as avian paradises. The lakes' shores and islands attract countless species of birds, making them hotspots for ornithological enthusiasts and researchers. Flamingos, pelicans, storks, herons, and a myriad of other bird species gather in these serene waters, turning the lakes into a living symphony of colors and calls.

Lake Nakuru's Pink Flamingos:

Lake Nakuru, in Kenya, is renowned for its breathtaking display of pink flamingos. These elegant birds flock to the lake's shallow alkaline waters to feed on algae, creating a surreal and mesmerizing spectacle. The sight of thousands of flamingos forming a delicate pink haze against the blue backdrop of the lake is a sight that captures the imagination and underscores the delicate balance of nature.

Lake Baringo's Biodiversity:

Lake Baringo, another jewel in the Rift Valley's crown, is an oasis of life surrounded by arid landscapes. This freshwater lake is home to a remarkable diversity of bird species, including the fish eagle and the Goliath heron. Crocodiles, hippos, and various fish species also call Lake Baringo home, showcasing the intricate web of life that flourishes in these waters.

Lake Turkana's Ancient Legacy:

Lake Turkana, also known as the Jade Sea, is not only the largest desert lake in the world but also a window into our ancient past. Its shores have yielded significant paleontological discoveries, including fossils of early hominids that offer insights into human evolution. The stark beauty of Lake Turkana's landscapes and the cultural heritage of the local communities contribute to its mystique.

Conservation Challenges:

The Rift Valley Lakes face challenges that threaten their delicate ecosystems. Human activities, including pollution, habitat degradation, and water extraction, can disrupt the balance of these natural wonders. Conservation efforts strive to mitigate these impacts and ensure the lakes' sustainability for future generations.

Balancing Conservation and Livelihoods:

Preserving the Rift Valley Lakes requires a delicate balance between conservation and the needs of local communities. Many people depend on the lakes for their livelihoods, engaging in fishing, agriculture, and tourism. Sustainable practices that protect the lakes' ecosystems while supporting the well-being of local residents are crucial for the long-term health of these fragile environments.

Ecological Resilience:

Despite the challenges, the Rift Valley Lakes exhibit a remarkable capacity for resilience. Many of these lakes are havens for biodiversity, showcasing the remarkable ability of nature to adapt and thrive even in the face of adversity. The lakes stand as a testament to the interconnectedness of life and the vital role that each species plays in maintaining the delicate balance of these ecosystems.

Continuing Reverence:

The Rift Valley Lakes are not just geological features or bodies of water—they are living legacies that inspire awe and reverence. They remind us of the delicate dance of life that unfolds on our planet and the importance of safeguarding these precious ecosystems for generations to come. As we gaze upon the serene waters and vibrant birdlife, we are invited to embrace our role as stewards of these ecological gems and avian paradises that grace the African landscape.

Injera and Berbere: Flavors of Ethiopia's Unique Cuisine

Ethiopia's cuisine is a tantalizing fusion of flavors, colors, and aromas that reflects the nation's rich history, cultural diversity, and resourceful ingenuity. Central to this culinary tapestry are two essential components: injera and berbere. In this chapter, we embark on a journey through the heart of Ethiopian gastronomy, exploring the art of injera-making and the vibrant world of berbere spice.

Injera: The Heartbeat of Ethiopian Meals:

Injera, often referred to as the "bread of Ethiopia," is more than just sustenance—it's a symbol of communal bonding and a cornerstone of Ethiopian cuisine. This unique flatbread is crafted from teff flour, a tiny grain native to the region. The fermentation process imparts a distinct tanginess to the bread, resulting in a slightly spongy texture that serves as an ideal vessel for savoring various dishes.

The Art of Injera-Making:

Injera-making is a revered culinary tradition that involves a careful balance of skill, patience, and artistry. The teff flour is mixed with water and allowed to ferment for a certain period, allowing the beneficial microbes to work their magic. The resulting batter is poured onto a large, flat griddle called a mitad, where it cooks into a delicate, lacy masterpiece. The injera is then stacked and served as a base for a variety of stews and dishes.

Berbere: The Soul of Ethiopian Spice:

No exploration of Ethiopian cuisine is complete without encountering berbere—a complex, fiery blend of spices that infuses dishes with depth, heat, and character. Berbere is a harmonious medley of ingredients, including red pepper, garlic, ginger, fenugreek, and more. The mixture is sun-dried and ground to a fine powder, releasing an intoxicating aroma that can transport diners to the heart of Ethiopian kitchens.

Berbere's Culinary Alchemy:

Berbere's role in Ethiopian cuisine is multifaceted. It's not merely a seasoning; it's a foundation that imparts a distinctive personality to a wide array of dishes. From stews like Doro Wat, a rich and spicy chicken dish, to lentil-based Misir Wat, berbere adds a fiery kick that stimulates the palate and creates a symphony of flavors. Its versatility allows it to elevate both vegetarian and meat-based offerings.

The Harmony of Injera and Berbere:

The pairing of injera and berbere epitomizes the essence of Ethiopian dining. Injera serves as a neutral canvas that absorbs the flavors of the accompanying stews, while berbere infuses each bite with a harmonious blend of heat and depth. This symbiotic relationship between bread and spice creates a sensory experience that transcends mere sustenance, inviting diners to engage with the meal on a profound level.

Cultural Significance and Traditions:

Injera and berbere are not just ingredients; they are woven into the fabric of Ethiopian culture. Sharing a communal platter of injera, topped with an array of flavorful stews, is a cherished tradition that fosters connections among family members and friends. The act of breaking bread and dipping injera into a shared dish creates a sense of unity and togetherness, reinforcing the importance of community bonds.

A Glimpse of Home:

For Ethiopians living abroad, injera and berbere offer more than just a taste of home; they evoke a sense of nostalgia and belonging. Ethiopian restaurants around the world proudly serve these iconic dishes, allowing both the diaspora and curious diners to experience a slice of Ethiopia's culinary heritage.

Safeguarding Tradition:

As the world becomes more interconnected, the flavors of Ethiopian cuisine have started to captivate global palates. The appreciation for injera and berbere underscores the importance of preserving traditional culinary practices while allowing for creative adaptations that respect the essence of the cuisine.

Culinary Identity in Every Bite:

Injera and berbere are more than elements of a meal—they encapsulate the soul of Ethiopian culinary identity. With every bite, the flavors of teff, spice, and tradition come together to create a symphony that resonates with both the senses and the spirit. As we indulge in injera and berbere, we embrace the richness of Ethiopia's culinary heritage, celebrating the marriage of simplicity and complexity that defines its unique cuisine.

Coffee Culture: From Legend to Global Bean

Coffee—much more than a beverage, it's a cultural phenomenon that has shaped societies, rituals, and interactions around the world. From its mystical origins in Ethiopia to becoming a global bean that bridges continents, this chapter delves into the captivating journey of coffee culture, from legend to cup.

The Ethiopian Legend:

The story of coffee's discovery is rooted in Ethiopian folklore. According to legend, a goat herder named Kaldi noticed his goats becoming unusually lively after nibbling on the red berries of a certain plant. Intrigued, Kaldi tried the berries himself and experienced a surge of energy. This tale of rejuvenation and discovery laid the foundation for what would become one of the world's most cherished beverages.

Birthplace of Coffee:

Ethiopia, often referred to as the "birthplace of coffee," has nurtured the cultivation and consumption of coffee for centuries. The coffee plant, known as Coffea arabica, thrives in the country's diverse climates and elevations. Ethiopians have woven coffee into their social fabric, transforming it into an integral part of their culture and traditions.

The Coffee Ceremony:

The Ethiopian coffee ceremony is a ritual that transcends mere caffeine consumption—it's a symbolic celebration of community, hospitality, and togetherness. The ceremony involves roasting green coffee beans, grinding them, and brewing the coffee in a traditional pot called a "jebena." The aromatic coffee is then poured into small cups, symbolizing the sharing of warmth and conversation.

Spread of Coffee Across Continents:

Coffee's journey from Ethiopia to the rest of the world began through trade routes and cultural exchange. By the 15th century, coffee had spread to the Arabian Peninsula, where it gained popularity in coffeehouses—a precursor to modern-day cafés. From there, coffee found its way to Europe, with Venice hosting the first European coffeehouse in the early 17th century.

The Rise of Coffeehouses:

Coffeehouses quickly became hubs of intellectual and social exchange. In Europe, these establishments facilitated discussions, debates, and the exchange of ideas among artists, writers, philosophers, and merchants. The emergence of coffeehouses marked a shift in public discourse and played a pivotal role in the Enlightenment.

Coffee and Colonization:

As European colonial powers expanded their global influence, they introduced coffee to regions beyond their borders. Coffee cultivation was established in colonies, including the Caribbean, Central and South America,

Africa, and Asia. The labor-intensive process of cultivating and harvesting coffee led to the establishment of plantations and shaped the socio-economic landscape of many regions.

Global Coffee Trade:

The 19th century witnessed the rise of coffee as a globally traded commodity. Coffee-producing countries became part of an interconnected supply chain, with beans journeying from plantations to international markets. The global demand for coffee led to economic growth for producing nations while fueling the appetites of coffee lovers worldwide.

Third Wave Coffee Movement:

In recent decades, a movement known as the "third wave" of coffee has emerged. This movement focuses on elevating coffee to an artisanal craft, emphasizing quality, sustainability, and the unique characteristics of different coffee varietals. Independent roasters and cafés champion the diversity of flavors found in different coffee-growing regions.

Cultural Fusion and Adaptation:

As coffee traveled the world, it evolved in response to local preferences and traditions. Various cultures developed their unique coffee beverages, from the strong espresso of Italy to the rich café au lait of France. Each adaptation reflects a fusion of global influences and local tastes, showcasing the diverse ways in which coffee has been embraced and integrated into different societies.

A Global Symbol of Connection:

Today, coffee stands as a universal symbol of connection—a thread that weaves through diverse cultures, languages, and landscapes. Whether sipped in a bustling café, shared during a traditional ceremony, or brewed at home, coffee embodies the art of coming together, exchanging stories, and forging bonds.

From Legend to Cup:

The journey of coffee from its humble beginnings to becoming a global phenomenon is a testament to its enduring allure. It has transformed from a mystical discovery in the Ethiopian highlands to a beloved beverage that transcends borders. As we savor each sip, we not only partake in the flavors of coffee but also engage in a centuries-old tradition that has united people across time and space.

Axum: Treasures of Aksumite Civilization

Nestled in the northern reaches of Ethiopia, the ancient city of Axum stands as a testament to the grandeur and achievements of the Aksumite civilization. This chapter embarks on a journey through time to explore the captivating history, monumental architecture, and enduring legacy of Axum—a city that once reigned as a powerful center of trade, culture, and innovation.

Historical Epicenter:

Axum's history stretches back over two millennia, making it one of the oldest continuously inhabited cities in Africa. It was the heart of the Aksumite Kingdom, a civilization that flourished from the 1st to the 7th century CE. The city's strategic location along trade routes linking Africa, Arabia, and the Mediterranean contributed to its prominence and prosperity.

Aksumite Achievements:

The Aksumite civilization was characterized by remarkable achievements that left an indelible mark on history. The kingdom's maritime prowess enabled it to dominate the Red Sea trade, establishing connections with ancient civilizations like Rome, India, and Persia. The city's impressive architecture, advanced coinage system, and distinctive stelae—all speak to the sophistication and ingenuity of the Aksumites.

Mystical Stelae:

Among Axum's most iconic features are its towering stelae, massive stone obelisks that served as both markers and monuments. These stelae, carved from single pieces of granite, are a testament to the Aksumites' architectural and engineering prowess. The tallest of them, the Obelisk of Axum, once stood at over 30 meters (98 feet) and weighed hundreds of tons—a testament to the scale of the civilization's ambitions.

Ark of the Covenant Legend:

Axum is shrouded in myth and legend, with one of the most enduring stories centering around the Ark of the Covenant. According to tradition, the Ark, containing the stone tablets of the Ten Commandments, was brought to Axum by Menelik I, the son of King Solomon and the Queen of Sheba. This tale underscores the city's role as a spiritual and cultural center.

Aksumite Religion and Culture:

The Aksumite Kingdom was a hub of cultural and religious exchange. The civilization's conversion to Christianity in the 4th century CE marked a pivotal moment in its history. The Church of St. Mary of Zion, believed to house the Ark of the Covenant, is a revered pilgrimage site for Ethiopian Orthodox Christians. The city's architecture and inscriptions also bear witness to its multicultural influences.

Decline and Resilience:

By the 7th century CE, the fortunes of Axum began to wane, influenced by factors such as shifting trade routes and the rise of Islamic empires. Despite this decline, Axum remained a center of influence in the Ethiopian highlands. The city's resilience is evident in its continued cultural significance and the endurance of its historical and architectural treasures.

Axum's UNESCO World Heritage Status:

Axum's significance has been recognized globally, with the city designated as a UNESCO World Heritage Site. This status acknowledges the exceptional value of Axum's historical and cultural heritage, as well as its contribution to the collective human story.

Rediscovering Axum:

In modern times, Axum remains a destination that enthralls visitors with its rich history and archaeological marvels. Exploring the ruins of the Great Stelae Field, marveling at the carved monoliths, and tracing the city's past through ancient inscriptions evoke a sense of connection to the past and a deep appreciation for the resilience of human civilization.

Legacy of the Ages:

Axum's legacy endures as a testament to the aspirations, achievements, and endurance of the Aksumite civilization. It stands as a link between past and present, a place where history whispers through the stones, and where the marvels of an ancient kingdom continue to captivate the imagination. As we walk the streets of Axum, we tread upon the echoes of a civilization that once shaped the course of history and enriched the tapestry of human culture.

Gondar's Royal Enclosure: Palaces and History

Nestled amidst the picturesque highlands of northern Ethiopia, Gondar's Royal Enclosure stands as a timeless testament to the grandeur and historical significance of the region. This chapter unveils the story of this regal complex, delving into the intricate architecture, storied history, and enduring legacy that make Gondar's Royal Enclosure a jewel in Ethiopia's historical crown.

Historical Background:

Gondar, often referred to as the "Camelot of Africa's Highlands," was established as the capital of Ethiopia in the 17th century by Emperor Fasilides. The Royal Enclosure, also known as the Fasil Ghebbi, emerged as the epicenter of the city's political, cultural, and architectural splendor. Its creation marked a departure from Ethiopia's traditional monastic architecture, as it embraced influences from various cultures, including India, Arabia, and Europe.

Architectural Marvels:

The Royal Enclosure is a captivating ensemble of palaces, castles, churches, and other structures that exemplify diverse architectural styles. The castles, often referred to as "fasilidas," showcase a fusion of Ethiopian design elements with foreign influences, resulting in a unique blend of forms, motifs, and materials. The structures are adorned with intricately carved details, symbolic motifs, and artistic flourishes that reflect the craftsmanship and vision of their creators.

Emperors and Empresses:

Throughout its history, the Royal Enclosure served as the residence and administrative center for a succession of Ethiopian emperors and empresses. These regal figures left their mark on the complex, each contributing to its expansion, enhancement, and cultural significance. Emperor Fasilides, who founded Gondar, set the stage for subsequent rulers to build upon his architectural vision.

Fasilides' Baths:

Among the most iconic features of the Royal Enclosure is Fasilides' Baths, a complex of pools and structures that served as a venue for the annual Timket (Epiphany) celebrations. During Timket, the baths are filled with water from the nearby Qaha River, and the faithful participate in a colorful and symbolic reenactment of Christ's baptism. The baths' design reflects a unique blend of spiritual symbolism and architectural innovation.

Emperor Yohannes I:

Emperor Yohannes I, known for his devout religious beliefs, made significant contributions to the Royal Enclosure. He constructed the imposing Palace of Emperor Yohannes I, a structure that epitomizes the fusion of indigenous Ethiopian architecture with foreign influences. The palace's ornate decoration and unique layout highlight the intersection of cultural and artistic influences.

Legacy and UNESCO Recognition:

The Royal Enclosure's significance transcends its historical role—it's a living testament to Ethiopia's cultural and architectural heritage. In recognition of its outstanding value, the site was designated as a UNESCO World Heritage Site in 1979. This status underscores the global significance of Gondar's Royal Enclosure as a repository of history, artistry, and human ingenuity.

Preservation and Restoration:

Efforts to preserve and restore the Royal Enclosure have been ongoing, aiming to safeguard its architectural treasures for future generations. The intricate process of restoration involves maintaining the original materials, techniques, and craftsmanship while ensuring the structural stability and aesthetic integrity of the complex.

Unveiling the Past:

Exploring the Royal Enclosure is akin to turning the pages of history, as each structure, carving, and courtyard unveils a new chapter in Ethiopia's story. The complex invites visitors to step back in time, to imagine the splendor of courtly life, and to appreciate the artistic genius that shaped its architecture.

Echoes of Royalty:

As we wander through the Royal Enclosure's corridors and courtyards, we are enveloped by the echoes of royalty, the whispers of past conversations, and the ambiance of imperial life. It's a journey that takes us beyond the physical structures, allowing us to grasp the spirit of the emperors, empresses, and artisans who crafted this architectural masterpiece—a testament to Ethiopia's rich history and enduring cultural identity.

Harar: East African Center of Trade and Learning

Nestled in the eastern part of Ethiopia, the ancient city of Harar stands as a crossroads of history, culture, and trade. This chapter embarks on a journey through time to uncover the rich tapestry of Harar's past—the convergence of civilizations, the legacy of learning, and the vibrant traditions that have shaped this unique city.

Historical Crossroads:

Harar's history is a tapestry woven with threads of diverse cultures and influences. Situated at the crossroads of major trade routes, the city has been a melting pot of civilizations for centuries. Arab, Indian, and African traders converged here, bringing with them a wealth of goods, ideas, and languages that enriched Harar's cultural mosaic.

The City of Gates:

Harar is often referred to as the "City of Gates," and for good reason. The city is encircled by a protective wall punctuated by five historic gates, each bearing its unique name and significance. These gates not only served as entry points but also symbolized the city's openness to diverse cultures and perspectives.

Harari Culture and Identity:

The inhabitants of Harar, known as Hararis, have cultivated a distinct cultural identity. The city's architecture, language

(Harari), and traditions reflect a blend of indigenous heritage and the influences brought by trade and interactions with other cultures. The Harari people have a long-standing tradition of weaving, metalwork, and intricate handicrafts that showcase their artistic prowess.

Harar's Learning Centers:

Harar has a rich history of intellectual and cultural vibrancy. The city has been a center of learning, attracting scholars and students from across East Africa and the Arabian Peninsula. The city's religious schools, or medresas, have played a pivotal role in preserving and disseminating knowledge, particularly in the fields of Islamic theology, philosophy, and literature.

Jugol: The Old Walled City:

The Jugol, Harar's historic old walled city, is a UNESCO World Heritage Site that encapsulates centuries of architectural and cultural evolution. The labyrinthine streets, traditional houses, and ornate mosques transport visitors to a bygone era. The layout of the Jugol is a reflection of the city's rich history, adapting to changing times while retaining its distinctive character.

Harar's Unique Architecture:

The architectural diversity of Harar is a testament to its multicultural past. The cityscape boasts traditional Harari houses with intricate woodwork and charming courtyards, alongside grand mosques with ornate minarets. The Rimbaud House, named after the French poet Arthur Rimbaud who lived in Harar, is another architectural gem that adds to the city's cultural tapestry.

The Coffee Connection:

Harar is also renowned for its unique coffee culture. The city's distinctive coffee beans, known as "Harari coffee," have gained international recognition for their distinctive flavors. Harar's coffeehouses, or "bunna bets," are gathering places where locals and visitors share stories, conversations, and the aromatic brew that has been a part of Harari life for generations.

Harar's Spiritual Heritage:

Religion has played a significant role in shaping Harar's identity. The city is home to over 80 mosques, which contribute to its reputation as an important center of Islamic culture and spirituality in East Africa. The Grand Jami Mosque, one of the city's oldest and most significant mosques, stands as a testament to Harar's religious heritage.

Cultural Diversity and Preservation:

Harar's cultural diversity is an ongoing source of pride and strength. Efforts to preserve the city's historic and cultural treasures, as well as its unique way of life, continue to be paramount. Harar's UNESCO designation underscores its exceptional value as a city where cultural exchange, historical significance, and vibrant traditions converge.

Harar: A Living Heritage:

As we traverse Harar's cobbled streets, immerse ourselves in its lively markets, and converse with its welcoming inhabitants, we experience a city that has retained its essence across the ages. Harar's vibrant past and present fuse seamlessly, creating an atmosphere where history, culture, and commerce intertwine. In Harar, East Africa's center of trade and learning, we discover a city that is as much a living museum as it is a vibrant, pulsating heart of Ethiopian heritage.

Addis Ababa: Journey Through the Capital's Evolution

Nestled within the Ethiopian highlands, Addis Ababa, meaning "New Flower" in Amharic, stands as a testament to Ethiopia's evolution, resilience, and modernity. This chapter embarks on a journey through time to explore the multifaceted history, cultural diversity, and dynamic growth that have shaped the capital city into a thriving metropolis.

Founding and Significance:

Addis Ababa's history is a relatively recent chapter in Ethiopia's narrative. Emperor Menelik II established the city in 1886, recognizing its strategic location and potential to serve as a neutral meeting ground for various ethnic groups. This founding not only marked the birth of a new urban center but also symbolized Ethiopia's intention to embrace modernity and connectivity.

Political and Diplomatic Center:

From its inception, Addis Ababa assumed political importance as Ethiopia's seat of government. The city became the administrative and diplomatic hub of the country, hosting important national institutions, embassies, and international organizations. The establishment of the African Union (AU) headquarters in Addis Ababa further solidified its role as a global diplomatic center.

Cultural Melting Pot:

Addis Ababa's growth has been fueled by the convergence of diverse cultures, languages, and traditions. The city's cosmopolitan character is a reflection of Ethiopia's multiethnic makeup, with residents hailing from various regions and backgrounds. This cultural diversity has enriched Addis Ababa's social fabric, contributing to a vibrant culinary scene, artistic expression, and communal celebrations.

Architectural Tapestry:

Addis Ababa's architectural landscape is a blend of historical and contemporary elements. The city boasts a mix of styles, from traditional Ethiopian design to modern high-rises. Historic landmarks such as the Menelik Palace, which served as the imperial residence, and St. George's Cathedral, a neo-Gothic masterpiece, coexist with modern landmarks like the African Union Conference Center and Millennium Hall.

Economic Growth and Infrastructure:

Over the decades, Addis Ababa has experienced substantial economic growth and infrastructural development. The city has become an economic powerhouse in the region, attracting domestic and foreign investment. Modern transportation systems, including the Addis Ababa Light Rail Transit, have improved connectivity and eased the city's traffic congestion.

Educational and Cultural Centers:

Addis Ababa's role as an educational and cultural hub is undeniable. The city is home to numerous universities, research institutions, and museums that contribute to Ethiopia's intellectual landscape. The Ethiopian National Museum, for instance, houses the famous fossil "Lucy," shedding light on the region's prehistoric past.

Urban Challenges and Sustainability:

As Addis Ababa continues to evolve, it faces urban challenges such as population growth, urbanization, and environmental sustainability. Efforts to balance modernization with preservation of cultural heritage and green spaces are ongoing, with initiatives aimed at sustainable urban planning, waste management, and conservation.

Celebrating Diversity:

Festivals and events in Addis Ababa celebrate the city's diverse heritage. The Meskel Festival, which marks the finding of the True Cross, and the Enkutatash Festival, celebrating the Ethiopian New Year, are just a few examples of the city's rich cultural calendar. These celebrations bring together residents and visitors to revel in the shared tapestry of traditions.

Addis Ababa's Future:

As Addis Ababa looks to the future, it continues to shape its identity as a dynamic capital city. Urban renewal projects, technological advancements, and investments in various sectors contribute to its ongoing transformation.

The city's aspiration to become a modern metropolis while preserving its historical essence speaks to Ethiopia's determination to embrace progress without forsaking its heritage.

An Ongoing Journey:

In Addis Ababa, a city whose name suggests new growth, we witness the fusion of history and modernity. It's a journey through Ethiopia's progress—a city that encapsulates the nation's journey from its ancient roots to its contemporary ambitions. The vibrant streets, the cultural diversity, and the bustling markets all reveal the dynamic spirit of Addis Ababa, a city that serves as a microcosm of Ethiopia's evolution.

Bahir Dar: Lake Tana's Monasteries and Blue Nile Majesty

Nestled along the shores of Lake Tana, the largest lake in Ethiopia, Bahir Dar is a city steeped in natural beauty, rich history, and cultural significance. This chapter invites you to embark on a journey to explore the serene allure of Lake Tana, the hidden treasures of its ancient monasteries, and the majestic splendor of the Blue Nile that cascades from its source nearby.

Lake Tana: Ethiopia's Azure Gem:

Lake Tana, known for its tranquil waters and shimmering expanse, occupies a central place in the heart of Bahir Dar. This vast lake, stretching over 80 kilometers (50 miles) in length, is not only a source of sustenance but also a sanctuary for unique flora, fauna, and a rich history that dates back centuries.

Island Monasteries: Preserving the Past:

Lake Tana is adorned with a collection of monastic islands, each hosting ancient churches and monasteries that have preserved Ethiopia's religious and cultural heritage. These monasteries, often accessible by boat, house priceless treasures such as illuminated manuscripts, religious artifacts, and vibrant murals that depict biblical scenes and stories.

Spiritual and Cultural Sanctuaries:

The island monasteries of Lake Tana serve as spiritual and cultural sanctuaries, offering a glimpse into the rich tapestry of Ethiopian Orthodox Christianity. The monastic life, rituals, and teachings have been passed down through generations, fostering a connection to a profound spiritual heritage that continues to resonate.

Ura Kidane Mehret: Jewel of Lake Tana:

One of the most renowned monasteries on Lake Tana is Ura Kidane Mehret. This monastery, dating back to the 16th century, is celebrated for its magnificent murals that depict scenes from the Bible and Ethiopian history. The circular church structure, adorned with colorful frescoes, stands as a testament to the artistic ingenuity of its creators.

Blue Nile Majesty: The Grand Abyssinia:

Beyond the tranquil shores of Lake Tana lies the source of one of the world's mightiest rivers—the Blue Nile. The Blue Nile, known as "Abay" in Amharic, begins its journey from the rugged landscapes near Bahir Dar. The Tis Issat Falls, commonly known as the Blue Nile Falls or "the Smoking Water," showcases the river's power and majesty as it thunders down a series of terraced cascades.

Natural Beauty and Biodiversity:

The Blue Nile Falls and its surroundings are not only a marvel of nature but also a habitat for a diverse array of flora and fauna. The lush landscapes, vibrant birdlife, and indigenous plants contribute to the area's ecological significance. The landscape has inspired generations of poets, writers, and artists who have attempted to capture its awe-inspiring beauty.

Development and Conservation: A Delicate Balance:

The allure of Lake Tana and the Blue Nile's beauty has attracted attention, leading to efforts to balance development with conservation. Initiatives focus on preserving the delicate ecosystems, promoting sustainable tourism, and safeguarding the historical and cultural treasures that adorn the region.

Exploring Bahir Dar: A Multi-Sensory Experience:

Bahir Dar is more than a gateway to Lake Tana and the Blue Nile—it's a city with its own distinct charm. The bustling markets, vibrant street life, and proximity to nature make it an appealing destination for travelers seeking both cultural immersion and natural beauty.

A Symphony of Elements:

As you stand by Lake Tana's shores, gazing at the timeless monasteries on the islands, or witnessing the thunderous spectacle of the Blue Nile Falls, you become a part of a symphony composed of water, history, spirituality, and natural wonder. Bahir Dar, with its deep-rooted history and breathtaking landscapes, invites you to embrace the serenity of its waters, the echoes of ancient prayers, and the magnificence of Ethiopia's blue and green treasures.

Historic Lalibela: Pilgrimage to Ethiopia's Spiritual Heart

Nestled in the rugged mountains of northern Ethiopia, Lalibela stands as a testament to human ingenuity, devotion, and spiritual significance. This chapter invites you to embark on a journey to the sacred city of Lalibela—a place of pilgrimage, architectural marvels, and profound religious devotion that has captured the hearts of both believers and admirers of history and art.

The Enigmatic Visionary: King Lalibela:

Lalibela's history is intertwined with the legacy of its namesake, King Lalibela. According to local tradition, King Lalibela was divinely inspired to create a "New Jerusalem" after a series of visions. With this divine guidance, he initiated the construction of a complex of rock-hewn churches that would not only serve as places of worship but also as a testament to his devotion and the spirituality of his people.

Astonishing Architecture: The Rock-Hewn Churches:

The rock-hewn churches of Lalibela are a marvel of human creativity and engineering prowess. Carved directly into the volcanic rock, these monolithic structures range in size and design, each with its unique characteristics. The twelve churches are divided into two main groups, symbolizing the earthly and heavenly Jerusalem, and they collectively comprise a UNESCO World Heritage Site.

Spiritual Significance: A Pilgrimage Destination:

Lalibela's significance extends beyond its architectural wonders—it's a pilgrimage destination of great importance. The city draws Ethiopian Orthodox Christians from across the country who embark on journeys to experience the spiritual aura of these sacred sites. The faithful believe that visiting Lalibela's churches during religious festivals or personal pilgrimages brings them closer to God and enhances their spiritual journey.

The Great Complex: Bete Medhane Alem:

At the heart of Lalibela's complex lies Bete Medhane Alem, the "House of the Savior of the World." This church is the largest monolithic rock-hewn church in the world, a colossal structure that awes visitors with its sheer size and intricate design. The interior features remarkable frescoes, murals, and architectural elements that reflect the artistic and spiritual devotion of its creators.

Spiritual Community: Living Faith and Tradition:

Lalibela is not just a historical relic—it's a living testament to Ethiopia's deep-rooted faith and tradition. The local community plays an integral role in maintaining and preserving the churches. Priests, monks, and the faithful are custodians of these sacred spaces, continuing the rituals, liturgies, and practices that have been passed down through generations.

Unveiling the Mysteries: Bet Giyorgis and Others:

Bet Giyorgis, or the Church of St. George, is perhaps the most iconic of Lalibela's churches. Carved in the shape of a cross, this church is a masterpiece of symmetry and elegance. Its design embodies profound symbolism, reflecting the cruciform shape of early Christian churches and paying homage to the enduring legacy of Ethiopia's Christianity.

Legacy and Preservation: Challenges and Triumphs:

Lalibela's status as a UNESCO World Heritage Site reflects its global significance and the need for its preservation. The city faces challenges such as erosion, weathering, and increasing visitor foot traffic. Preservation efforts are focused on using traditional techniques and modern conservation practices to ensure that these extraordinary structures remain intact for future generations to experience and cherish.

Beyond the Rocks: Exploring Lalibela's Soul:

Lalibela's spiritual essence extends beyond its rock-hewn churches. The city's religious festivals, including Timket and Meskel, provide opportunities to witness vibrant processions, traditional music, and communal celebrations that capture the heart of Ethiopian spirituality. The local way of life, the hospitality of the people, and the surrounding landscapes add layers of depth to the pilgrimage experience.

A Journey of the Spirit:

As you step into the hallowed grounds of Lalibela, you embark on a journey that transcends time and space. The whispers of prayers, the echoes of footsteps, and the reverence of pilgrims unite to create an atmosphere that is both mystical and tangible. Historic Lalibela, with its rock-hewn churches and spiritual significance, offers an opportunity to connect with Ethiopia's spiritual heart—a place where devotion and creativity coalesce into an enduring testament of faith and human achievement.

Danakil Depression: Unveiling Earth's Harshest Beauty

Nestled in the northeastern corner of Ethiopia, the Danakil Depression is a landscape unlike any other—a paradox of stark harshness and breathtaking beauty. This chapter takes you on a journey into the depths of the Danakil Depression, where a symphony of extremes unfolds, revealing the power of geological forces and the resilience of life in one of the most inhospitable environments on Earth.

A Geologist's Playground:

The Danakil Depression is a geological marvel—a showcase of tectonic activity and the forces that shape our planet's surface. Located at the junction of three tectonic plates, the depression is characterized by its active volcanoes, geothermal springs, and salt formations. This dynamic landscape is a testament to the Earth's ever-changing nature.

The Lowest Point in Africa:

One of the Depression's most iconic features is the Dallol volcano, which holds the distinction of being one of the hottest and lowest places on the planet. The Dallol volcano sits at approximately 116 meters (381 feet) below sea level and boasts acidic hot springs, colorful mineral deposits, and striking salt formations that create an otherworldly tableau of colors.

The Spectacle of Salt:

The Danakil Depression is renowned for its vast salt flats, stretching across the landscape like a glistening white sea. The salt formations, known as "salt pans" or "salt flats," are created by the evaporation of ancient saltwater lakes. These salt flats are not only visually captivating but also hold immense economic importance as a source of salt extraction for the region.

The Sulphurous Symphony:

The Danakil Depression is a land of paradoxical beauty—an environment of extreme temperatures and conditions that nurture unique forms of life. Sulphur deposits around the Dallol volcano create vibrant hues of yellow, green, and red, painting the landscape with an eerie and captivating palette. The smell of sulphur hangs in the air, a sensory reminder of the Earth's primordial forces.

The Afar People: Life in the Extreme:

Despite the harsh conditions, the Afar people have thrived in the Danakil Depression for generations. These resilient inhabitants have adapted to the demanding environment, utilizing its resources for survival. Salt mining and trade, as well as nomadic herding, are integral parts of their way of life, showcasing the remarkable resilience of humanity in the face of adversity.

Erta Ale: Gateway to the Abyss:

Erta Ale, meaning "smoking mountain" in the local Afar language, is a continuously active shield volcano that has captured the fascination of adventurers and scientists alike.

Its summit crater houses one of the world's few lava lakes—a mesmerizing pool of molten rock that offers a rare glimpse into the Earth's fiery core.

Scientific Insights: Studying Earth's Processes:

The Danakil Depression isn't just a visually stunning landscape—it's also a scientific treasure trove. Researchers and geologists flock to this unique environment to study tectonic processes, volcanic activity, and extremophile life forms that have adapted to thrive in the most challenging conditions.

A Precarious Balance:

The Danakil Depression is a landscape in constant flux—a dynamic equilibrium between creation and destruction, beauty and hostility. The forces that shape the Depression remind us of the Earth's geological heritage and the fragility of our planet's surface. This extraordinary environment serves as a reminder of the awe-inspiring power of nature and the intricate interplay of Earth's systems.

Unveiling Nature's Extremes:

The Danakil Depression invites us to witness nature's most extreme expressions—the searing heat, the explosive energy, and the unexpected vibrancy of life in seemingly uninhabitable conditions. It's a place where harshness and beauty coexist, offering a unique perspective on the boundless diversity and resilience of our world. As you journey through the Danakil Depression, you become an explorer of Earth's harshest beauty, immersing yourself in a realm that pushes the boundaries of what we know and understand about our planet.

Conclusion

The journey through the history, culture, and landscapes of Ethiopia has been a tapestry woven with threads of ancient civilizations, vibrant traditions, and breathtaking beauty. From the origins of humanity in the Afar region to the soaring obelisks of Aksum, the rock-hewn wonders of Lalibela, the resilient spirit of Addis Ababa, and the captivating landscapes of the Danakil Depression, Ethiopia's story is one of resilience, diversity, and profound significance.

As we conclude this exploration, it becomes clear that Ethiopia's history is a testament to the enduring legacy of its people. From the rise and fall of kingdoms to the struggles against colonization and occupation, Ethiopia's journey is marked by its determination to maintain its identity and sovereignty. The cultural mosaic that makes up the Ethiopian tapestry is a blend of diverse ethnic groups, languages, and faiths, all contributing to a rich heritage that is celebrated and preserved.

The chapters of this book have taken us through Ethiopia's spiritual heart in Lalibela, the echoes of its ancient script and Coptic Christianity, the vibrant celebrations of festivals like Timket, and the culinary delights of its unique cuisine. We've delved into the challenges faced during the Italian-Ethiopian War and the Derg regime, as well as the triumph of independence for Eritrea and Ethiopia's emergence as a modern nation.

Throughout this journey, Ethiopia's connection to its land and heritage has been evident. The towering mountains, verdant valleys, expansive lakes, and rugged deserts have served as the backdrop for human history and natural wonders. Ethiopia's landscapes are as diverse as its people, offering a canvas of beauty and intrigue that captures the imagination.

From the heart of Lalibela's rock-hewn churches to the depths of the Danakil Depression's extreme landscapes, Ethiopia's story is one of contrasts, complexities, and constant evolution. The chapters of its history have been marked by conquests, triumphs, spiritual devotion, and a continuous drive for self-determination. As we close this book, it's evident that Ethiopia's narrative is far from complete—its people continue to shape their nation's destiny, honoring their past while forging a future that is uniquely Ethiopian.

The pages of this book offer only a glimpse into the rich tapestry of Ethiopia's history and culture. Its story is ongoing, its chapters are still being written, and its contributions to the world continue to unfold. As we bid farewell to this journey, may the echoes of Ethiopia's past and the promise of its future resonate in the hearts and minds of those who have embarked on this exploration.

Thank you for taking the time to immerse yourself in the rich history, culture, and landscapes of Ethiopia through the pages of this book. I hope that this exploration has been as enlightening and captivating for you as it has been for me to share it with you.

If you've enjoyed delving into Ethiopia's ancient past, vibrant traditions, and diverse landscapes, I kindly ask for your support. Your positive review would mean the world to me and would help others discover the wonders of Ethiopia's story.

Your feedback and encouragement inspire me to continue sharing the world's diverse and fascinating narratives. As you reflect on the chapters you've journeyed through, I hope you're inspired to explore and appreciate the beauty of Ethiopia even more.

Thank you once again for being a part of this journey. Your engagement and enthusiasm mean everything to me.

Made in the USA
Monee, IL
11 January 2026

41391024R00066